THE
HINDU JAJMANI SYSTEM

THE HINDU JAJMANI SYSTEM:

A SOCIO-ECONOMIC SYSTEM INTERRELATING MEMBERS OF A HINDU VILLAGE COMMUNITY IN SERVICES

WILLIAM HENRICKS WISER

GYAN

Published by

Gyan Publishing House
5, Ansari Road
Daryaganj, New Delhi-110002
Phone: 011-47034999, 9811692060
E-mail: books@gyanbooks.com

Distribution Network
gyanbooks.com
India, USA, Canada, UK, Australia

ISBN: 978-93-7014-336-4 (PB)

First Published, 1936

2nd Impression 2025

Printed at: Gyan Press, Delhi.

THE HINDU JAJMANI SYSTEM
Author: WILLIAM HENRICKS WISER

THE HINDU JAJMANI SYSTEM

A SOCIO-ECONOMIC SYSTEM INTERRELATING MEMBERS OF A HINDU VILLAGE COMMUNITY IN SERVICES

BY

WILLIAM HENRICKS WISER, M.A., Ph.D.
(Co-author "Behind Mud Walls")

LUCKNOW PUBLISHING HOUSE
LUCKNOW, U.P., INDIA
1936

CONTENTS

CONTENTS

PREFACE

IN October 1925, while engaged in Christian rural social service for the North India Mission of the Presbyterian Church of the U. S. A., my wife and I were permitted to become camp residents of a village which we call Karimpur. It has a population of 754, consisting mostly of farmers, is located 27° 19′ N. and 79° 8′ E., in the United Provinces of India, and lies in the fertile area between the Ganges and Jumna rivers. For centuries it has been in the possession of, or under the direct influence of, Brahmans, and furnishes an excellent center for the study of a long-established Hindu village community. Various missionaries of the North India Mission had had occasional contacts with the village over a period of not less than sixty years. Ours was the unique privilege, for the purpose of study, of spending all our time in this one village of five consecutive camping seasons and of retaining intimate contacts with it until March 1931, from our residence at Mainpuri, five and one-half miles distant. A brief sketch of the village and of the people living in it, with some of our personal experiences, are given in our book entitled "Behind Mud Walls".

While in the village we heard for the first time the terms "Jajman"* and "Jajmani* Haqq." Gradually we discovered that these terms referred to an established service relationship which was somewhat like the old feudal system, yet unlike it. It contained a mutuality that was lacking in the feudal system. With the help

*Pronounced "judg-mann" and "judg-mann-e."

of two Hindu youths, Nawal Behari and Bajrang Pande, we were able gradually to aeeumulate the information whieh is given in the following pages. This study was finally prepared during residenee in Cornell University under the helpful guidance of Professors Sanderson, Eaton and Boyle.

Students of the Indian village community, like Baden Henry Baden-Powell and Sir Henry Sumner Maine, have been interested more in the blood-relationship and land-tenure rights than in problems of soeial inter-relationship of the villagers. Students of the Hindu caste system have been interested in origins and easte distribution. Students of Indian rural economics like Gilbert Slater, Sir Henry Sumner Maine, and Radhakamal Mukerjee have reeognized the presence of an intrieate pattern of every day relationships, but no one has made an attempt to reeord these relationships. Gilbert Slater writes, "Various strands of economie, social and religious eonditions are strangely and deftly interwoven in the web of South Indian life, and low wages, low effieiency, and high abstinence are the ground plan of the pattern." (Page 17, "Some South Indian Villages"). Sir Henry Sumner Maine says, "Nothing can be more eomplex than the customs of an Indian village, though in a sense they are only binding on ehiefs of families. The examination of these eustoms, whieh have for their objeet to seeure a self-aeting organization not only for the eommunity as a whole, but for the various trades and eallings which fraetions of it pursue, does not fall within the seope of the present leeture, but it is a subjeet full of interest." (Page 117, Sir Henry Sumner Maine, "Village Communities in the East and West"). Radhakamal Mukerjee writes, "In India, where soeiety was not organized after the feudal pattern, the development of the guilds partook of the nature and process of fission and absorption, giving to each group its rights and privileges which were protected by the established traditions of voluntary social co-operation." (Radhakamal Mukerjee, "Democracies of the East," page 293).

References to the term "jajman," or "jujman" as it is spelled in older literature, are found in court records usually in reference to the employer of a Brahman priest. The priest is referred to as the "purohit" and his rights as "purohiti haqq." We have discovered in Karimpur, however, that the term "jajman" is used for all who have the employer relationship. And the rights involved in the employer-employee relationship are popularly called "Jajmani haqq." Just how general this "Jajmani" relationship is in the villages of India we are not prepared to state. The fact that Slater, and Pandian in "Indian Village Folk" refer to the different services in South India, and Altekar in his chapter on "Village Occupations" in a "History of Village Communities in Western India" refers to the "servants of the community" indicates that there is in existence in other parts of India something similar to what we find in North India. Just what it is called in the different vernaculars we do not know.

It is hoped that this analysis of the Hindu Jajmani system as found in a North India village will lead to further studies of a similar sort in other parts of India. These materials will then afford a basis for comparative studies for students of economics, sociology, politics and philosophy in an analysis of what Mukerjee calls the "Communal-Conservative" type of village community.

W. H. Wiser

June 1, 1936 Saharanpur, U. P., India

FOREWORD

THIS second edition of *The Hindu Jajmani System* by William H. Wiser will be welcomed by all students of Indian society and culture. Based upon field work and a thorough knowledge of the village community. Wiser's little book is in the best anthropological tradition and an important contribution to our scientific knowledge of Indian village life.

Although first published 22 years ago, Wiser's work is still the only detailed analysis of the *jajmani* system and represents the first attempt to present as a system, the complex exchanges of goods and services between castes. It provides us with a framework for a better understanding of much discrete data which earlier observers, such as Russel, Crooke, Baden-Powell, Ibbetson and Darling, described under the heading "village menials", "village servants", artisans, *jajmans*, *kamins*, etc. It also facilitates detailed comparative analysis and the application of modern sociological rôle theory to the relationship between *jajman* and *kamin*.

In focusing upon the economic aspects of the caste system, Wiser has done pioneer work; for despite the abundant literature on caste, its economic aspects have been relatively neglected. An awareness of the relationship between caste and economy seems to be missing even in such a standard book as J. H. Hutton's *Caste in India* (Oxford University Press) in the revised edition of which (1951) there is no reference to the *jajmani* system or to Wiser's work. Most books on caste have dealt with the problems of its historical origins and development, with the rules governing endogamy, food taboos, ritual purity and caste ranking, and the more dramatic injustices of untouchability. It is common in works about caste for the author to list the castes of a particular region with some account of the traditional occupation of each; but it is a curious fact that the author generally avoids what might logically seem to be a next step, an analysis of how these groups interact with one another in the production and exchange of goods and services.

When Wiser wrote his book he did not know how general or widespread this system might be, although he referred to some passages in the works of other writers which suggested that it had a wide range of diffusion. This conclusion is supported by more recent studies, which give evidence for much of the same kind of system in eastern Uttar Pradesh, parts of Malabar and Cochin, Mysore, Tanjore, Hyderabad, Gujarat, and the Punjab.

Wiser's definition of the *jajmani* system stresses the element of reciprocity between *jajman* and *kamin* and the stabilizing and integrating aspects of the system, but his data also points to the asymmetrical nature of the power relationship. Landownership is clearly the single most important determinant of power in the *jajmani* system. Indeed, a major function of the system is to assure a stable labour supply for the dominant agricultural caste in a particular region by limiting the mobility of the lower castes, especially those who assist in agricultural work. In spite of Wiser's essentially benevolent interpretation of the *jajmani* system he is not unaware of the harsh realities inherent in the hierarchical patterns of village life. This awareness is given sharp expression in his book *Behind Mud Walls*, written in collaboration with his wife, Charlotte Viall Wiser.

> "The leaders of our village are so sure of their power that they make no effort to display it. The casual visitor finds little to distinguish them from other farmers .... And yet when one of them appears among men of serving caste, the latter express respect and fear in every guarded word and gesture. The serving ones have learned that as long as their subservience is unquestioned the hand which directs them rests lightly. But let there be any move toward independence or even indifference among them, and the paternal touch becomes a strangle-hold .... n every detail of life have the leaders bound the villagers to themselves. Their favour may bring about a man's prosperity and their disfavour may cause him to fail, or may make life so unbearable for him that he will leave the village." (pp. 18-19).

That the ownership of land, including house sites, is the crucial factor in power position of the *jajman*, appears in other areas as well. "In the good old days," writes Darling of the Punjab, "village servants were in complete subjection to their 'masters', and this is still largely the case in the feudal north and west. There the fear of ejection from the village is a yoke which keeps the head bowed, and only those who own their own house and courtyard dare assert themselves." (M. L. Darling. *Wisdom and Waste in the Punjab*, Oxford University Press, 1934, p. 272.) "That the *zemindar* is all-powerful in such places need hardly be stressed," writes Mohinder Singh. "The threat of demolishing a man's dwelling or ejecting him therefrom are powerful weapons in his hand for extorting *begar*. Till recently the cultivators did not have any rights in their house sites." (M. Singh, *The Depressed Classes*, Hind Kitabs, Bombay, 1947, p. 35.)

While the landowners are generally of higher caste in Indian villages, it is their position as landowners, rather than caste membership *per se*, that gives them status and power. In Karimpur, where the Brahmans are the land-owners, the traditional caste hierarchy obtains. But in Rampur the Jats own the land, and the Brahmans are subservient to them. Majumdar and his colleagues present a similar picture in their description of the village near Lucknow: "The respect which the Brahmans enjoy is merely conventional; in daily life, however, the Brahmans are treated on an equal footing with the other castes . . . The Thakurs are the most influential group of people in the village because they are economically better off. They own most of the agricultural land in the village. They are the landlords who give employment to the other caste people. The various other castes serve the Thakurs as their dependents." (D. N. Majumdar, *et al.* "Intercaste relations in Gohanakallan, a village near Lucknow," *Eastern Anthropologist*, Vol. 8, p. 211, 1955).

Since the passing of *Zamindari* Abolition Bills, the key power of landowners may have been curtailed in certain areas. Majumdar and his colleagues, for example, report in the village they studied near Lucknow, where *Zamindari* abolition has taken place, Camars now refuse to perform *begar*, while the barbers refuse to draw water for the Thakurs and will not wash their utensils or remove their leaf-plates any more. (D. N. Majumdar, *ibid*, pp. 191-92). However, the occurance of *begar* since Indian independence has been noted in some areas—by Gitel Steed, for example, and by Shridar Misra. "Caste Survey in two modal villages with stereotyped discriminations," in *Intercaste*

Tensions, University of Lucknow, mimeographed, 1951, p. 58.)

It is true that while a landowner may have both tenants and *kamins*, the two groups need not be identical. He may have *kamins* who are not his tenants. This point is made by Opler and Singh, who also note that when there are disputes between Thakurs, the tenants align themselves with their landlords. (M. Opler and R. D. Singh. "The Division of Labour in an Indian Village", in *A Reader in General Anthropology*, C.S. Coon, Ed. Holt, New York, 1948, pp. 464-496.) Perhaps a more crucial consideration, however, is that the Thakurs in Senapur, like the Jats in Rampur, form a caste group that may (despite factional cleavages and wealth differences) join ranks in solidarity *vis-a-vis* the lower castes in crucial issues.

The lower castes, theoretically at least, have a potential retaliatory weapon in the boycott, or withdrawal of their services. Thus, when the Nais of Rampur were informed of a decision of the Jats to reduce the *neg jog* paid at weddings, they stopped shaving and cutting their *jajman's* hair in protest. But the sequel is instructive. The Jats retaliated by buying razors and shaving themselves. This shows that such protests may prove to be self-defeating. It also indicates that the *jajmani* system may be disrupted by action of either the *jajmans* or the *kamins*, or by the cumulative effect of both. (See Lewis and Barnouw "Caste and the *Jajmani* System in a North Indian Village", *Scientific Monthly*, Vol. 83, No. 2, August 1956.)

Since Wiser first published his book in 1936 the *jajmani* system has been weakened by far-reaching social, economic and political changes in India. Among the most important changes have been the increasing population pressure on limited land resources, the *zamindari* land reforms, the trend from a subsistence to a market economy, accompanied by the greater use of money in the villages, increased off-farm employment, the introduction of labour saving devices, the spread of education, the campaigns against untouchability, and the general strengthening of the position of some of the lower castes. Despite these forces, the *jajmani* system is still an important feature of village life. However, the weakening of the system has led to increased hostility and open violence between castes in many parts of the country and has been disruptive of traditional village unity. Perhaps the new tensions are part of the birth pangs of a new and more democratic social order. Certainly it is difficult to reconcile the semi-feudal, hierarchical values of the *jajmani* system with the expressed ideals of Indian leaders for a modern democratic nation. Moreover, it must never be forgotten that the vaunted unity of the much idealized traditional Indian village, was generally based upon the coercive power of the landholding *jajman*.

Oscar Lewis
Department of Anthropology and Sociology
University of Illinois

INTRODUCTION

IN a Hindu village in North India each individual has a fixed economic and social status, established by his birth in any given caste. If he is born into a carpenter family, he finds himself related by blood to carpenters exclusively. All of his paternal and maternal relatives in that village or in other villages are members of the carpenter caste, and that alone. The men folk in all of these families earn their livelihood through the carpentry trade, sometimes supplemented by agriculture. Each carpenter has his own clientele, which has become established through custom, and which continues from generation to generation. Where the village is large enough, the clientele will be limited by the boundaries of the village. If the village is not large, or the members of carpenter families are too numerous to meet the needs of one village, the clientele extends to small neighbouring villages where there are no carpenters in residence. This relationship once established cannot be broken except by the carpenter himself who may choose to sell his rights to another carpenter. It is heritable and sometimes transferable.* The relationship fixes responsibilities both on the carpenter and the one whom he serves. The carpenter during the sowing season must remove and sharpen the plough point once or twice a week. During the harvest he must keep sickles sharp and renew handles as often as demanded. He must be ready to repair a cart whenever called upon by a customer, or to make minor repairs on the customer's house. In exchange he receives at each harvest, twenty-

*See Indian Law Reports Vol. XLIII, page 35.

eight pounds of grain, for every plough owned by his client. Additional rights and responsibilities will be described later.

This service relationship is established not only between carpenters and other residents of the village, but affects all castes. Each caste in the village at some time during the year is expected to render a fixed type of service to each other caste. As there is no exact equivalent of this system in the West, it will be necessary to use the terms in current use in North India. The carpenter calls his entire clientele his "jajmani" or "birt"—these terms being identical in meaning. The individual family or head of the family whom the carpenter serves is called the carpenter's "jajman." The "jajman" speaks of the carpenter's family and all other families that serve him as his "Kam-wale" *or "Kam karne-wale"* (*i. e.* workers), if they are of the serving castes, *i.e.*, Sudras or lower. If the one who serves is a "Pandit" (title for a Brahman priest), a "Bhat" (astrologer), or another from one of the three upper caste divisions, he is referred to by his caste name—"Pandit," "Bhat," etc. and not as a "kam-karne-wale."

There are twenty-four different castes in Karimpur.* In their order of social precedence and traditional occupation they are as follows:

1. Brahman—priest and teacher
2. Bhat—family bard and genealogist.

} Brahman and related

*Pronounced "Käm-wäley" or "Käm-ker-ney-wäley."

*The term "caste" is being used as applying to all residents of the village. In terms of religion it cannot be applied to the Bhangis who are Christians, or to the Faqirs, Manihars, Dhunas, and Tawaif, who are Mohammedans. But in terms of occupation and in village parlance these groups are referred to as castes and are listed above as such.

3.	Kyasth—accountant	Kshatriya and related
4.	Sunar—goldsmith	
5.	Mali—florist	Sudra
6.	Kachhi—Vegetable grower	
7.	Lodha—rice-grower	
8.	Barhai—carpenter (One family does iron-smithy work and is called Lohar—iron worker, although not of that caste)	
9.	Nai—barber	
10.	Kahar—water-bearer	
11.	Gadariya—shepherd	
12.	Bharbhunja—grain parcher	
13.	Darzi—seamster	
14.	Kumhar—potter	
15.	Mahajan—tradesman	
16.	Teli—oil presser	
17.	Dhobi—washerman	outcaste
18.	Dhanuk—mat maker	
19.	Chamar—leather worker	
20.	Bhangi—sweeper and cesspool cleaner	
21.	Faqir—hereditary Mohammedan beggar	
22.	Manihar—Mohammedan glass bangle seller	
23.	Dhuna—Mohammedan cotton carder	
24.	Tawaif—Mohammedan dancing girl	

A social organization, such as the Hindu caste system, which gives each occupational group a fixed standing within the community, must of necessity have certain patterns of behaviour which enable each caste to maintain its own status and satisfactorily engage in relationships with others. Among these behaviour patterns are marriage, social intercourse in matters of eating, drinking and smoking, conventions of untouchability and unapproachability and service interrelationships with which we are concerned in this study. We find therefore that in the service interrelationships, except where social disabilities arise, as in the cases of the lower castes and non-Hindus, such as Mohammedans, each caste renders service, within the range noted below, limited or unlimited, to each of the other castes.

	Occupation	*Is served by castes*	*Serves castes*
1.	Priest and teacher	1—24	1—19
2.	Bard and genealogist	1—24	1—19
3.	Accountant	1—24	1—24*
4.	Goldsmith	1—24	1—24
5.	Florist	1—24	1—24
6.	Vegetable grower	1—24	1—24
7.	Rice grower	1—24	1—24
8.	Carpenter (iron-worker)	1—24	1—24
9.	Barber	1—24	1—15, 22, 23
10.	Water-bearer	1—24	1—19
11.	Shepherd	1—24	1—24
12.	Grain parcher	1—24	1—24
13.	Seamster	1—24	1—24
14.	Potter	1—24	1—24
15.	Tradesman	1—24	1—24
16.	Oil presser	1—24	1—24
17.	Washerman	1—24	1—19, 21—24
18.	Mat maker	1—24	1—24
19.	Leather worker	1—24	1—24

*As the servant of Government.

	Occupation	*In served by castes*	*Serves castes*
20.	Sweeper and cesspool cleaner	4—8, 11—16, 18—24	1—24
21.	Mohammedan beggar	4—24	1—16, 21—24
22.	Mohammedan glass bangle seller	4—24	1—24
23.	Mohammedan cotton carder	4—24	1—24
24.	Mohammedan dancing girl	4—24	1—16, 21—24

Actually we find the following service relationships. Table I reveals variations which will be better understood as one proceeds with the study. These service relationships reveal that the priest, bard, accountant, goldsmith, florist, vegetable grower, etc., etc., are served by all of the other castes. They are the jajmans of these other castes. In turn each of these castes has a form of service to perform for the others. In this manner the various castes of a Hindu village in North India are interrelated in a service capacity. Each serves the others. Each in turn is master. Each in turn is servant. Each has his own clientele comprising members of different castes which is his "jajmani" or "birt." This system of interrelatedness in service within the Hindu community is called the Hindu "Jajmani system."

TABLE

ANALYSIS OF INTER-SERVICE

No.	Name of caste	SERVED
		Fixed Relationship
1	Priest and teacher ...	1, 2, 5, 8-10, 12-14, 16-22 ...
2	Bard and genealogist ...	1, 5, 8-10, 12, 14, 16-22 ...
3	Accountant ...	1, 2, 5, 9, 10, 12, 14, 16-19, 21, 22...
4	Goldsmith ...	1, 2, 5, 9, 10, 12, 14, 16-22 ...
5	Florist ...	1, 2, 8-10, 12, 14, 16, 18-22 ...
6	Vegetable grower ...	1, 2, 5, 6-10, 12, 14, 16-19, 21, 22 ...
7	Rice grower ...	1, 2, 5, 8, 10, 12, 14, 16, 18, 19, 21, 22 ...
8	Carpenter-iron worker ...	1, 2, 5, 9, 10, 12, 14, 16-19, 21, 22...
9	Barber ...	1, 2, 5, 10, 12, 14, 16, 18-22 ...
10	Water-bearer ...	1, 5, 8, 9, 12, 14, 16-19, 21, 22 ...
11	Shepherd ...	1, 5, 8, 9, 10, 12, 14, 16-19, 21, 22...
12	Grain Parcher ...	1, 5, 14, 16, 18, 19, 21, 22 ...
13	Seamster ...	1, 5, 9, 12, 14, 16-19, 21, 22 ...
14	Potter ...	1, 5, 9, 12, 16, 18, 19, 21, 22 ...
15	Tradesman ...	1, 5, 8, 9, 12, 14, 16, 18, 19, 21, 22...
16	Oil Presser ...	1, 5, 8, 10, 12, 14, 17-19, 21, 22 ...
17	Washerman ...	1, 5, 12, 14, 16, 18, 19, 21, 22 ...
18	Mat Maker ...	1, 5, 8, 12, 14, 16,17, 19, 21, 22...
19	Leather worker ...	1, 5, 8, 12, 14, 16, 17, 21, 22 ...
20	Sweeper and Cesspool cleaner.	5, 12, 14, 16, 22 ...
21	Mohammedan Beggar ...	5, 8, 12, 14, 16, 17, 19, 22 ...
22	Mohammedan Glass Bangle Seller	5, 8, 9, 12, 14, 16, 19, 21 ...
23	Mohammedan Cotton Carder	5, 8, 9, 12, 14, 16, 19, 21, 22 ...
24	Mohammedan Dancing Girl	5, 12, 14, 16, 19, 21 22 ...

I.

Relationship in Karimpur

By Castes	Serves Castes.	
Casual Relationship	Fixed Relationship	Casual Relationship
3, 4, 6, 7, 11, 15, 23, 24 ...	1-19 ...	—
3, 4, 6, 7, 11, 13, 15, 23, 24	1, 3-9 ...	10-19
4, 6-8, 11, 13, 15, 20, 23, 24	—	1, 2, 4-24 (1)
3, 6-8, 11, 13, 15, 23, 24	—	1-3, 5-24
3, 4, 6, 7, 11, 13, 15, 23, 24	1-4, 6-24 ...	—
3, 4, 7, 11, 13, 15, 20, 23, 24	—	1-5, 8-24
3, 4, 6, 11, 13, 15, 20, 23, 24	—	1-6, 8-24
3, 4, 6, 7, 11, 13, 15, 20, 23, 24	1, 2, 5-7, 10, 11, 15, 16, 18, 19, 21-23	3, 4, 9, 12, 13, 14, 17, 20, 24
3, 4, 6-8, 11, 13, 15, 23, 24	1-6, 8, 10, 11, 13-15, 22, 23 (2)	—
2, 3, 4, 6, 7, 11, 13, 15, 20, 23, 24	1-9, 11, 16 ...	12-15, 17-19
2-4, 6, 7, 13, 15, 20, 23, 24,	—	1-10, 12-24
2-4, 6-8, 10, 11, 13, 15, 20, 23, 24	1-11, 13-24 ...	—
2-4, 6-8, 10, 11, 15, 20, 23, 24	1 ...	2-12, 14-24
2-4, 6-8, 10, 11, 13, 15, 20, 23, 24	1-13, 15-24 ...	—
2-4, 6, 7, 10, 11, 13, 20, 23, 24	—	1-14, 16-24
2-4, 6, 7, 11, 13, 15, 20, 23, 24	1-15, 17-24 ...	—
2-4, 6-8, 10, 11, 13, 15, 20, 23, 24	1-4, 6, 8, 10, 11, 13, 16, 18, 19, 21 (3)	—
2-4, 6, 7, 10, 11, 13, 15, 23, 24	1-17 ...	—
2-4, 6, 7, 10, 11, 13, 15, 23, 24	1-18, 21-24	—
3, 4, 6-8, 11, 13, 15, 23, 24	1, 2, 4, 5, 9 ...	3, 6-8, 10-17
3, 4, 6, 7, 11, 13, 15, 23, 24	1-19, 22-24 ...	—
3, 4, 6, 7, 11, 13, 15, 23, 24	1-21, 23, 24 ...	—
3, 4, 6, 7, 11, 13, 15, 24	—	1-22, 24
3, 4, 6-8, 11, 13, 15, 23	—	1-23

(1) As Government Officers.
(2) Others with exception of sweeper and Mohammedan beggar shaved by outside barbers.
(3) Other with exception of sweeper cared for by outside washerman.

In return for the various services rendered, there are payments in cash and in kind made daily, monthly, bi-yearly, per piece of work, and on special occasions, depending on the type of service rendered and in part on the goodwill of the jajman. The strength of the system depends, however, not on the actual payments made but on the concessions granted to the different occupational groups. These may be listed as:

a. Free residence site
b. Free food for family
c. Free clothing
d. Free food for animals
e. Free timber
f. Free dung
g. Rent-free land
h. Credit facilities
i. Opportunities for supplementary employment
j. Free use of tools, implements and draft animals
k. Free use of raw materials
l. Free hides
m. Free funeral pyre plot
n. Casua lleave
o. Aid in litigation
p. Variety in diet
q. Healthful location

These concessions do not apply equally to all, but vary according to custom. The value of the concessions to the average man in any given group is so great that without hesitation he turns down a fixed cash income that may be offered to him by a mill employer in a neighbouring city.

INTRODUCTION

The Hindu Jajmani system has philosophical and religious sanction in the Laws of Manu which have served as guide for the Hindu social and economic organization for almost 2,000 years. The Laws of Manu* (Chap. I, Verses 87—91) state:

> "But in order to protect this universe He, the most resplendent one, assigned separate (duties and) occupations to those who sprang from his mouth, arms, thighs and feet. To Brahmanas he assigned teaching and studying (the Veda), sacrificing for their own benefit and for others, giving and accepting (of alms). The Kshatriya he commanded to protect the people, to bestow gifts, to offer sacrifices, to study (the Veda), and to abstain from attaching himself to sensual pleasure. The Vaisya to tend cattle, to bestow gifts, to offer sacrifices, to study (the Veda), to trade, to lend money, and to cultivate land. One occupation only the lord prescribed to the Sudra, to serve meekly even these (other) three castes."

Where necessity arises the castes may assume the duties of the caste next lower to them. (See Manu X: 81-100), but they may never "live by the occupation of a higher one". "The king shall deprive of his property and banish (X: 96)" anyone who presumes to do this. Again, "he who lives according to the law of another (caste) is instantly excluded from his own. (X: 97)". Finally, we find in Chapter XII of the Laws of Manu, the following threats for those who do not meet their responsibilities.

> "But (men of the four) castes who have relinquished without the pressure of necessity their proper occupations, will become the servants of Dasyus, after migrating into despicable bodies. (70) A Brahmana who has fallen off from his duty (becomes) an Ulkamukha Preta, who feeds on what has been vomited; and a Kshatriya, a Kataputana (Preta) who eats impure substances and corpses. (71) A Vaisya who has fallen off from his duty be-

*See The Sacred Books of the East, Vol. XXV, Edited by Max Muller, Published by Oxford University Press.

comes a Maitrakshagyotika Preta, who feeds on pus; and a Sudra, a Kailasaka (Preta), who feeds on moths. (72)."

The Jajmani system has, within the past 150 years, been further strengthened by civil law. That which was formerly a custom sanctioned by religion has been recognized by the English courts in India. In reversing a judgment releasing a jajman from his responsibilities,

> "The Sitting Judge (G. Giberne) held that the Zillah (District) Judge had taken an erroneous view of the subject, and that his decision had tended to upset a custom universally acknowledged, and endangered the constitution and foundation of all village communities established from time immemorial. The Sitting Judge was satisfied with the evidence taken before the Moonsiff (Judge) and considered the Bullootteedars (workers) were entitled to their hucks (rights) from every villager, according to the rules of the village communities; and that if the villagers declined to employ their services, to which they were entitled, they must still pay the Bullootee hucks" (rights to share on crops).* (Case No. 1,489, 29th September, 1840—Bombay Sudder Dewanee Adawlut compiled by A. F. Bellasis.)

It is impossible to have an adequate understanding of the system without studying the interrelationships that have been established among the different groups in the intricacies of their community life. These group relationships will be analyzed in the first section by a description of the functional responsibilities of each caste; in the second section by a description of the means of realization and the means of maintenance of the compensations and rights of the castes; and in the third section by a description of the disintegrating factors in the caste interrelationships. We will then be in a position to evaluate the system.

*See Altekar "History of Village Communities in Western India", page 92 ff on the *Balute* system.

SECTION I

Jajmani Functional Responsibilities in Karimpur

AT the present time (1932), members of twenty-four castes are living in Karimpur. They are engaged in their hereditary services which, with few exceptions, are all that are necessary to meet the needs of a self-sufficing community. The different castes will be considered in their order of social precedence, as recognized in the village. It may be well to note here that every village in North India does not have identical services available within its village boundaries. Karimpur lacks the services of a weaver, a sweetmaker, a dyer, etc., etc. Another village may lack a potter, a cotton carder, a goldsmith, an oil presser, etc., etc. In that case these services are rendered by members of the particular caste which is performing them in some adjoining village, and with whom a jajmani or a purely commercial relationship may be established. Our chief concern is not to establish the fact that in this year 1932 every village in North India has twenty-four castes rendering services such as are noted in the introduction, but to establish the fact that there is today within a North India Hindu village community an interrelation of services which carries with it certain responsibilities and rights. These responsibilities and rights constitute the structure of the Hindu Jajmani system. As the various factors are analyzed, it becomes evident that we have here a system which is very similar to or identical with the religio-socio-economic plan of occupations outlined two thousand years ago by Hindu philosophers and law-makers.

1. THE BRAHMAN.* (*Priest and Religious Teacher*)

The Laws of Manu, Chapter 1: 93 state:

> "As the Brahmana sprang from (Brahman's) mouth, as he was the first born, and as he possesses the Veda, he is by right the lord of this whole creation."

Again,

> "To Brahmanas he assigned teaching and studying (the Veda), sacrificing for their own benefit and for others, giving and accepting (of alms)." (I:88) "He who, being (duly) chosen (for the purpose), performs the Agnyadheya, the Pahayagnas, (and) the (Srauta) sacrifices, such as the Agnishtoma (for another man), is called (his) officiating priest." (I:143)....."Teaching, studying, sacrificing for himself, sacrificing for others, making gifts and receiving them are the six acts (prescribed) for a Brahmana (X:75). But among the six acts (ordained) for him three are his means of subsistence, (viz) sacrificing for others; teaching and accepting gifts, from pure men" (X:76).

Thus we find the Brahman, or Brahmana as given in the Laws of Manu, established in the highest position of Hindu society as one who is to serve as a teacher of the holy books and as officiating priest. The Laws of Manu, Chapter X: 1, safeguard the position of the Brahman by stating, "Let the three twice-born castes (varna), discharging their (prescribed) duties, study (the Veda), but among them the Brahmana (alone) shall teach it, not the other two; that is an established rule". Every faithful Hindu if he is going to meet the requirements of his religion must be taught the sacred books by a Brahman and must have his religious sacrifices administered by a Brahman.

---

*Pronounced "Brăh-mun".

JAJMANI FUNCTIONAL RESPONSIBILITIES

In actual practice in Karimpur today, we find the Brahmans functioning to a very small degree as teachers, and scholars, but maintaining to a higher degree their hereditary position as priests—sacrificing for themselves and for others. Religious teaching in the village is controlled by the Brahmans. Secular teaching is controlled by an outside body, the District Board, which follows a Government Code. The introduction of secular education has made it possible for children to learn their letters from secular teachers, who may or may not be Brahmans. This opportunity for contact with the child in the elementry learning is now lost to the village Brahman teacher. The child does not tend to accept the teachings of a local untrained religious teacher after having been taught by a trained secular teacher who comes in from the outside. His religious training is now an indirect rather than a direct process. Parents and travelling religious ascetics pass on to him traditions through song and story. Teachers in Government and private schools familiarize him with the sacred books in their daily religious exercises. Other ideas reach him through participation in the activities of special religious ceremonies and feast days.

The Brahman, however, still maintains his right to function as family-priest. He alone may recite sacred texts, make the various offerings, and officiate at all ceremonies of a formal religious nature, such as the Investiture of the Sacred Thread for the Twice-Born, weddings, deaths, special religious festivals, and the recitation of sacred books. There is no temple in Karimpur, hence no temple-priest.

In 1925, 187 of the 754 residents of Karimpur—about one fourth—were Brahmans. They represented 41 out of the 161 families in the village. (The family being the group that eats from one and the same *chulha i.e.* hearth fire.) Of these 41 families, only three families were practicing the traditional work of priesthood, and only one of these was making his livelihood from this work exclusively. The 41 families represent seven sub-castes, which in order of precedence are: *Chaube* (3), *Pande* (31), *Misur* (1), *Dube* (2), *Tanguriya* (1), *Tiwari* (1), *Mahere* (1) and *Dogli* (1). The three families engaged in priesthood are *Chaube, Misur* and *Tiwari.* The *Chaube* family which is highest in the social scale, serves twenty-six *Pande* families and the *Misur* family. The three *Chaube* families, in order to have a priest of a higher sub-caste, call in a priest from an adjoining village. The *Misur* family serves five *Pande* families, two *Dube* families, one *Tanguriya* family, one *Tiwari* family, one *Mahere* family, the *Dogli,* one bard family, one Kshatriya accountant family, one florist family, sixteen vegetable growers' families, one rice grower family, one barber family, one water-bearer family, one grain parcher family and three potter families—a total of thirty-seven families. The *Tiwari*—a lone man—serves the remaining seventy-three families that are entitled to the services of a Brahman priest. The twenty-one sweeper and Mohammedan families are too low to ask for the services of a priest.

We find then that the priesthood needs of the village are met as follows:—

3 *Chaube* families by an outside priest.
27 Brahman families by the *Chaube* family.
37 families by the *Misur* family.
73 families by the *Tiwari* priest.
21 families without the services of a priest.

161 families—total.

JAJMANI FUNCTIONAL RESPONSIBILITIES

The unequal division of patrons as shown above, is counter-balanced by economic factors. The 27 families represent largely the rich, the 37 families the middle class and the 73 families the poor. The rich make more frequent calls on their priest than do the middle class, and the middle class make more calls than do the poor. In this manner each priest has very nearly an equal number of calls made upon his time. The calls made by the greater numbers of poor for weddings and deaths is counter-balanced by the calls of the smaller number of the rich for special religious celebrations which the poor cannot afford. These factors tend to equalize the income received by each priest.

The question now arises as to what happens to the 38 Brahman families who are not needed as priests or teachers. The Law of Manu provides occupations for them.

> "A Brahmana must seek a means of subsistence which either causes no, or at least little, pain (to others), and live (by that), except in times of distress. (IV: 2). For the purpose of gaining bare subsistence, let him accumulate property by (following those) irreproachable occupations (which are prescribed for) his (caste), without (unduly) fatiguing his body, (IV:3).
>
> "He may subsist by Rita (truth), and Amrita (ambrosia), or by Mrita (death) and by Pramrita (what causes many deaths); or even by (the mode) called Satyanrita (a mixture of truth and falsehood), but never by Svavritti (a dog's mode of life) (IV:4).
>
> "By Rita shall be understood the gleaning of corn; by Amrita, what is given unasked; by Mrita, food obtained by begging; and agriculture is declared to be Pramrita. (IV:5).
>
> "But trade and (money-lending) are Satyanrita, even by that one may subsist. Service is called Svavritti; therefore one should avoid it. (IV:6)......Moreover, among these four Brahmana householders each latter (named in next verse) must be considered

more distinguished, and through his virtue to have conquered the world more completely. (IV:8.)

"One of these follows six occupations (gleaning corn, acceptance of gifts given unasked, begging, agriculture, trade and teaching), another subsists by three (accepting gifts, sacrificing, teaching), one by two (sacrificing and teaching), but the fourth lives by the Brahmasattra (teaching) (VI:9)."

Again in Chapter X:

"Among the several occupations, the most commendable are, teaching the Veda for a Brahmana, protecting (the people) for a Kshatriya, and trade for a Vaisya, (X:80)......But a Brahmana unable to subsist by his peculiar occupations just mentioned, may live according to the law applicable to Kshatriyas, for the latter is next to him in rank. (X:81)......If it be asked, 'How shall it be, if he cannot maintain himself by either (of these occupations)?', the answer is, he may adopt a Vaisya's mode of life, employing himself in agriculture and rearing cattle. (X:82)."

We find therefore that although teaching and sacrificing are the highest forms of occupation for Brahmans, when necessity arises they may engage themselves as warriors, agriculturists, cattle raisers and traders. As warriers are not usually necessary in a peace loving community, we find our Brahman families engaged in agriculture. A few of them supplement their earnings by raising cattle—not for beef. The one *Tanguriya* family keeps a small shop where one may buy a few spices, grain and tobacco.

By becoming successful farmers the 38 Brahman families may be classed as householders, so highly commended by Manu.

"Because men of the three (other) orders are daily supported by the householder with (gifts of) sacred knowledge and food, therefore (the order of) householders is the most excellent order. (III:78)."

They can assure those who serve them of a decent livelihood and fulfil one of their many obligations.

> "They (the Brahmans) must allot to him out of their own family (property) a suitable maintenance, after considering his ability, his industry, and the number of those whom he is bound to support. (X:124)".

They do not lose their status in the community when they do not serve as priests and teachers. The Laws of Manu state:

> "Thus, though Brahmanas employ themselves in all (sorts of) mean occupations, they must be honoured in every way; for (each of) them is a very great deity. (IX:319)".

They can help Sudras to fulfil their highest destiny.

> "But let a (Sudra) serve Brahmanas either for the sake of heaven, or with a view to both (this life and the next); for he who is called the servant of a Brahman thereby gains all his ends. (X:122). The service of Brahmanas alone is declared (to be) an excellent occupation for a Sudra; for whatever else besides this he may perform will bear him no fruit. (X: 123)".

And finally Brahmans themselves can attain to *Brahma.*

> "That Brahmana who thus daily honours all beings, goes, endowed with a resplendent body, by a straight road to the highest dwelling place (*i. e. Brahman*). (III: 93)".

We find then that the responsibilities of the Brahman as recognized in Karimpur today are essentially the same as they were two thousand or more years ago. Those Brahmans necessary to perform the priestly functions of the community are found in three families. The remaining 38 Brahman families maintain their prestige by abstention from forbidden occupations and by providing less favoured castes with an opportunity to work out their salvation.

2. The Bhat*. (*Bard and Genealogist*)

The Bhat stands next to the Brahman in the social scale. In Karimpur they are called Rae, and they function as bards at weddings. Bates' Hindu Dictionary defines Bhat as being "a certain tribe of bards; a bard, minstrel, panegyrist, a genealogist or family bard." The two Bhat families are engaged in agriculture. The senior men of the two families are present in most of the village councils and although often called upon for information regarding the past, do not stand out as being different from the other agriculturists of the village. Their talk and interest centers about agriculture.

But when a wedding occurs they assume a new importance. They are one of the three castes which may serve as messengers between the bride's and the groom's people, and are active in helping to keep things running smoothly. At the proper moment the Bhat whose right it is to serve the particular family, recites a poem telling of the virtues of the bride and groom. There is no demand for the special services of these men except at weddings, and at that time the poem is not an essential part of the ceremony. Were either of the men outstanding in their poetic ability there would be numberless calls for them, because listening to poetry is one of the favourite pastimes of the Indian. The Bhats of Karimpur are not gifted as poets. In actual practice, members of the first eight caste groups, only, call for the services of the Bhat. And the Bhat does not urge the necessity of his services, unless an occasion is such that a share in it will add to his social prestige. If an ambitious family below the social level of the first eight groups wants the services of a Bhat in making

*Pronounced Bhat.

a wedding really impressive, it must make an alluring offer before the Bhat will be interested. The rights of the two Bhat families in the village are divided roughly between the east and the west side, and are equally valuable.

Traditionally the Bhat stands next to the Brahman in the social scale because he is generally "supposed to be descended from the intercourse of a *Chattri* and a Brahman widow." (Vol. II, page 20, "Tribes and Castes of the North West Province and Oudh" by W. Crooke.) This ancestry gives him a standing higher than that of his father who came from the second great caste division—the *Kshatriya*, and lower than that of his mother who came from the highest division—the Brahman. According to the Laws of Manu, Chapter X:11, the offspring of a *Kshatriya* with a Brahman woman is a *Suta* and Chapter X:47 assigns to *Sutas* the "management of horses and of chariots". In Karimpur neither the above stated hereditary name, nor occupation, is held by the two Bhat families.

3. The Kyasth*. (*Accountant*)

Next in the Karimpur social scale is the Kyasth. The head of the one Kyasth family serves the District Revenue Officers as *patwari* (village accountant) in a nearby village. As a member of the Hindu caste system and as a resident of the village, he gives support to the Jajmani system on an asymmetrical basis. He himself renders no specific occupational service other than what he is expected to do as a government officer. Like the other better class families in the village he is able to share his earnings with those in the village who have services to render. One Kyasth from an adjoining village, who serves as patwari in Karimpur, sometimes resides in the village.

*Pronounced Kí-ásth ("a" as in "abound").

The Kyasth is the sole representative of the *Kshatriya* caste, the second great division of the Hindu system. According to the Laws of Manu, the *Kshatriya* was:

> "Commanded to protect the people, to bestow gifts, to offer sacrifices, to study (the Veda), and to abstain from attaching himself to sensual pleasures. (I:89)......The seniority......of Kshatriyas is from valour (I:155)......Let him know that these (following) are the four means for securing the aims of human (existence); let him, without ever tiring, properly employ them. (VII: 100) What he has not (yet) gained, let him seek (to gain) by (his) army; what he has gained, let him protect by careful attention; what he has protected, let him augment by (various modes of) increasing it; and what he has augmented, let him liberally bestow (on worthy men). (VII: 101).....To carry arms for striking and for throwing (is prescribed) for Kshatriyas as a means of subsistence......but their duties are liberality, the study of the Veda, and the performance of sacrifices. (X:79)."

We learn from the above that by heredity the *Kshatriya* was allotted the military services of the Hindu system. Kings as well as soldiers were *Kshatriyas.* When aggression was necessary the army of the *Kshatriyas* was responsible. In times of peace they were responsible for protecting the members of the Hindu system, and especially the Brahmans.

> "Not to turn back in battle, to protect the people, to honor the Brahmanas, is the best means for a king to secure happiness, (VII: 88)......But (a king who feels his end drawing nigh) shall bestow all his wealth, accumulated from fines, on Brahmanas, make over his kingdom to his son, and then seek death in battle. (IX: 323)...A king who (duly) protects (his subjects) receives from each and all the sixth part of their spiritual merit; if he does not protect them, the sixth part of their demerit also (will fall on him) (VIII: 304).....A king who does not afford protection, (yet) takes his share in kind, his taxes, tolls and duties, daily presents and fines, will (after death) soon sink into hell. (VIII 307)."

The Kshatriya is not only responsible for the safety of members of the Hindu system but he is likewise expected to take a large share in keeping the caste system rigid.

> "(The king) should order a Vaisya to trade, to lend money, to cultivate the land, or to tend cattle, and a Sudra to serve the twice-born castes. (VIII: 410)......(A king) who knows the sacred law must inquire into the laws of castes (gati) of districts, of guilds, and of families, and (thus) settle the peculiar law of each. (VIII: 41)......By taking his due, by preventing the confusion of the castes (varna) and by protecting the weak, the power of the king grows, and he prospers in this (world) and after death. (VIII: 172). .. ..When the Kshatriyas become in any way overbearing toward the Brahamanas, the Brahmanas themselves shall duly restrain them, for the Kshatriyas sprang from the Brahmanas, (IX: 320). Kshatriyas prosper not without Brahmanas; Brahmanas prosper not without Kshatriyas; Brahmanas and Kshatriyas being closely united, prosper in this (world) and in the next. (IX: 321)."

The *Kshatriyas* did not hold their position as military protectors for the Hindu system for a very long time. About the 11th century "the great political event of the period was the rise of the Rajputs as warriors in the place of the Kshatriyas. Their origin is obscure but they appeared in the 8th century and spread from their original homes in Rajputana and Oudh, into the Punjab, Kashmir, and the Central Himalayas assimilating a number of fighting clans and binding them together with a common code." (*Times of India* Year Book 1931, page 55) The Census of India 1931, Vol. XVI, page 221, states that "The representatives of the second division of Manu (the Kshatriyas) according to the universal opinion at the present day in these provinces are the Rajputs, Thakurs and Chattris." We find therefore that in the United Provinces, the *Rajputs* replaced the *Kshatriyas* in service and have become identified with the second great caste division. Further on, the Census Report states that the Kyasths are included among those "who claim to be Kshatriyas and who are considered to be of high social standing, though their claim is not universally admitted." (page 222) Their lack of traditional function seems to have made them unstable socially.

In the Hindu code the *Kshatriyas* did not lose their standing in the social caste system, but they ceased to function as warriors. The Laws of Manu provided for such an emergency by allowing the *Kshatriyas* to seek livelihood in any form other than that prescribed for the Brahman. "A Kshatriya who has fallen into distress may subsist by all these (means); but he must never arrogantly adopt the mode of life (prescribed for his) betters." (X: 95).

The *Kshatriyas* were employed by the Mohammedan and English rulers as revenue agents or "writers", hence we find them until recently occupying most of the positions of this kind. The *Kyasth* or *Kshatriyas* families which have a relationship to the village at the present time, function not as community agents but as agents of the government in control. Their relationship to the village has been described in the opening paragraph.

4. The Sunar*. (*Goldsmith*)

The Sunars of Karimpur belong to the *Chattri* sub-caste of Sunars and as such "are probably the same as the Tank Sunars of the Punjab, who profess to be degenerate Kshatris or Aroras," (Crooke, "Tribes and Castes of the North West Province and Oudh," IV, p. 334.) They rate socially just a little lower than the Kshatriya. Strictly speaking, the goldsmith has no fixed jajmans, as most other castes in the village have. His contribution to the life

*Pronounced "Soo-när".

of the village is not an absolute necessity. Residents of the village may or may not have jewelry made. They usually purchase jewelry at the time of a wedding. In addition they may have some made from time to time from the little savings which they prefer to store in the form of jewelry. The Sunar cannot control this demand or require people to patronize him. When they do patronize him he has an opportunity to show his artistry. He is prepared to do four classes of work; (1) *Sada*, plain gold or silver bangles without ornamentation; (2) *Chitai*, net work which includes designs of flowers; (3) *Jarao* or *Murassa*, all work involving the setting of stones and raised and joined work; (4) *Jaldar*, filigree work.

The Sunar has been listed as serving all castes in the village. He does do so on occasions, but not of necessity. Where a whole community like Karimpur is jajmani-minded, the goldsmiths have built up for themselves a semi-jajmani relationship, and they have many regular voluntary patrons. There are many villagers who would not think of going to the town or city for their jewelry. If the village goldsmith cannot make for them the particular designs they desire, they authorize him to go to the town or city as their agent to make the purchase. Our local goldsmiths, however, can meet the demands made by most of their patrons.

On the other hand, there are residents in Karimpur who have begun to take advantage of transportation facilities and venture to the cities to make their purchases where they claim they can get better rates. They represent the few bolder spirits in the village who are prepared to run the risk of being robbed of their silver as they travel to the city, of being fleeced by shrewd goldsmiths when they arrive, and of being relieved of the jewelry on their return journey home. These residents feel no obligation to their local goldsmiths, and if questioned, will give as a reason for not patronizing them, the goldsmith's roguery.

Most goldsmiths have found it worth their while to move into market towns, official centers and industrial centers, where the demand for their services is more constant. But there are still villages, such as Karimpur, where one may find goldsmiths. The two families in Karimpur, in addition to being gold and silver smiths, engage in money-lending, pawn-broking, and the purchase of old jewelry. The earnings from these sources have not sufficed, and we find that within the past few years the Sunars have supplemented their earnings by engaging in agriculture.

The Sunars, like the Kshatriyas, Bhats and Brahmans furnish the patronage for other services in the village, hence do their bit in the maintenance of a village community. Were it not for this group of substantial residents, the village could not claim so many serving castes, and, were it not for the varied services of these serving castes, a few like the Sunars would move elsewhere.

5. The Mali*. (*Florist*)

The Mali, florist or horticulturist, is the highest of the Sudra castes living in Karimpur. According to the Laws of Manu, "a Sùdra whether bought or unbought, he (the Brahmana) may compel to do servile work; for he was created by the self-existent (Svayambhu) to be the slave of a Brahmana. (VIII; 413)." They are probably descended from the "original inhabitants (of the country) ...or the following inhabitants of the forest. (viz.) hunters,

*Pronounced "Mä-lee".

fowlers, herdsmen, fishermen, root-diggers, snake-catchers, gleaners, and other foresters (those who collect flowers, fruit and fuel). (VIII: 259, 260)."

The original inhabitants of the country were fitted into the Aryan system and assigned definite services to be rendered to the three higher castes. It cannot be assumed that all Sudras are pure descendants of the original inhabitants. Many of them are the descendants of mixed marriages between Aryans and Aborigines. For that reason one does not find universality of castes of Sudras throughout India. Sir Henry Sumner Maine in "Village Communities in the East and West" states:

> "There is only one perfect universal caste, that of the Brahmans; there are a certain number of isolated dynasties and communities pretending to belong to the second of the theoretical castes; but in the enormous majority of instances caste is only the name for a number of practices which are followed by each one of a multitude of groups of men, whether such a group be ancient and natural, or modern and artificial. As a rule, every trade, every profession, every guild, every tribe, every clan is also a caste, and the members of caste not only have their own special objects of worship selected from the Hindoo pantheon or adopted into it, but they exclusively eat together and exclusively intermarry. (Page 218-220)."

One probable reason for the high standing of the Mali is that he supplies the proper flowers or leaves for the formal religious ceremonies. He supplies the headdress for the bridegroom and garlands for the bride and groom and their relatives. He supplies the leaves that are necessary for the marriage booth. He supplies the flowers for the ceremony on the 13th day after his jajman's death. He supplies the flowers for the *Chhati* and *Mul Shant* ceremonies after the birth of a child. He supplies the mango leaves, flowers and the fuel for the sacred fire for the investiture of the sacred thread ceremony. In every formal ceremony in which the priest officiates, the Mali is required to supply flowers or leaves and fuel for the sacred fire. He keeps a garden from which he gets his supply of wood, leaves and flowers. In addition he always has a supply of *Mendhi* (Lawsonia inermis), or henna, the leaves of which are used for making the red colour rubbed on the soles of the feet, on the toe-nails and finger-nails of the bride and groom, and on the head where the hair is parted, for the bride. The demand for henna is not limited to weddings since the women find frequent occasion to beautify themselves with it.

The one Mali family of Karimpur has as its jajmans everyone in the village and the residents of all of the neighbouring hamlets.

6. The Kachhi*. (*Vegetable Grower*)

The Kachhis, or vegetable growers, are the traditional agriculturists of the village. Although nearly all castes in Karimpur engage in a certain amount of agriculture, the Kachhis are the specialists. They can make crops and vegetables grow where no one else can. Their old men pass on to the young men the hard-earned traditional methods of agriculture. The more prosperous Brahman farmers in the village like to reduce the risks of farming by getting Kachhis to take a share in the growing of certain crops.

The Kachhis were probably among the earliest farmers in this part of India. At that time they were not dependent upon the services of others. It did not worry them if they had to go without a shave or if the dirt stains

*Pronounced "Kä-chhee".

remained in their hastily washed clothes. They needed no carpenters to fashion their tools. There were among them as there still are, some who could use an adze. They had their own bards and were content to eat from leaf platters of their own making and sit on palm leaf mats of their own weaving. But now this is all changed. They have been welded into the Hindu religious-social-economic order and are expected to share in maintaining its strength.

They play their part dutifully, but while doing it, fail to conceal the spirit of independence which has always been theirs as conquerors of the soil. The Hindu system has given them no exclusive economic rights, since every caste is now engaged in agriculture. However, they hold their own economically by being superior to the other agriculturists. They excel especially in their ability to grow vegetables. They supply vegetables to anyone in the village who desires them. If there is no market for them in the village, the Kachhis know where they can sell them—in some other village or at one of the many fairs or special markets. The only matter in which they show marked dependence, is that of financial credit. This dependence was probably developed and encouraged by the Aryan invaders, as we have observed in parts of the country where Aryans are newly arrived. The Kachhis represent the best risks in the village. And furthermore cheap credit is a successful method of gradually transferring assets away from credulous sons of the soil.

The twenty-six Kachhi families have gained a fixed status in the Hindu social order—that of being among the highest of the Sudra castes and jajmans of numerous services. One after another the Kachhis have accepted the services offered to them by the various occupational castes and they together with the Brahman, Bhat and Kyasth families make a solid foundation for a jajmani system with its many diversified services.

7. THE LODHA* (*Rice Grower*)

What has been written about the Kachhi could be written about the Lodha or rice grower. As there is only one family in the village ve.y little is seen or heard of them, especially since they devote all of their time to agriculture. The Lodha like the Kachhi is an agriculturist. The Kachhi has won a special reputation for growing vegetables, and the Lodha for growing rice. The Lodha is not the only one who grows rice. Men of all castes engaged in agriculture now grow rice although the early history of the village might have shown divisions in the growing of crops. The Lodha like the Kachhi is independent. He is willing to sell rice or grain to those who want it and he takes his place among those who support the Hindu socio-economic system. A number of Lodha families live in a hamlet a mile distant. They depend on Karimpur for a number of services.

8. THE BARHAI†. (*Carpenter*)

THE LOHAR‡. (*Iron-Worker*)

Chief among the essential artisans in the village are the Barhais or carpenters. They rank next to Kachhis and Lodhas in the Karimpur social scale. For the mud houses of the village they make the doors, door frames, and stairways, and fashion joists, threshold planks, wall

*Lodha—pronounced "Lò-dhä."

†Pronounced "Burr-hígh".

‡Pronounced "Lo-här".

pegs and water spouts. For the agricultural implements they make the implement handles, plough beams, bodies, shares, yokes, mallets and plank harrows. For the household they make bread boards, rolling pins, degchie (cooking vessel) covers, platters, charpai (rope bed) frames, pestles for crushing grain, small eating platforms, large platforms (used for general sitting purposes), fodder cutting stumps, water jar stands and boxes for storing clothes. For miscellaneous purposes, they make frames for wells, well wheels, wheel supports, weighted beams for small wells, cart wheel rims, spokes and hubs, cart bodies, cane press poles and bases, and sandals. They do the tree cutting in the village and saw up the timber for their own use.

One may judge from the above list, the importance of the carpenter in this village community. Eight carpenter families supply the needs of Karimpur and adjoining hamlets. Most of the work done is of a seasonal nature. During the sowing season, they are busy with the ploughs of their jajmans; during the harvest, they give their time to sickle making and repairing. When the rushed times are over, they occupy themselves with other repairs, yokes, carts, doors and door frames for one or all of the four big fairs which give them a market for their goods. They also engage in a certain amount of agriculture. Like the Kachhis, they are constantly occupied.

As a result of the large amount of work to be done, one family has specialized in iron work. The man of this family is usually referred to as the "Lohar"—ironworker. There are special castes engaged in iron work alone, of which one is the Lohar caste. But as there are no representatives of these castes in the village, the carpenter engaged in their work is given their name. One group of true Lohars wander about, gypsy-fashion, and occasionally visit Karimpur. They do heavy work such as making sledge-hammers, crow-bars and anvils. Occasionally smaller things are made by them if there is no one on hand to supply the articles locally. The local carpenter-iron-worker makes the plough shares, spuds, spades, fodder choppers, and sickles that are in most frequent use in the village.

The Barhai's relationship to his jajmans is fixed by the number of ploughs owned by each of them. If the jajman owns one plough he has to pay a fixed rate, as mentioned in the next section. In return for this rate the Barhai must keep the plough in constant repair. And repairs on a village plough are frequently necessary. If the jajman owns two ploughs, the rate paid to the carpenter is doubled. Jajmans who do not own ploughs have more of a trading relationship with the carpenter. An assessment of the value of the jajmani rights of each carpenter family is made in the third section of this study.

9. The Nai*. (*Barber*)

The Nai, or barber, who stands next in the Karimpur social scale is considered by the villagers to be chief among the local menials. Shaving and cutting hair is just "busy work" for the barber, to keep him from sitting idle when he is not running errands for his numerous jajmans. The barber carries the invitations for all auspicious ceremonies of significance held in the homes of his jajmans. He spends much time in going from village to village to carry personal messages to the relatives of his jajmans. He is always the bearer of good news. Seldom is he called upon to carry the news of a death. This is usually done by an outcaste.

*Pronounced "Nígh-ee".

JAJMANI FUNCTIONAL RESPONSIBILITIES

The barber is expected to shave each one of his prominent clients, such as the village elders, twice a week. Once a week, on Wednesdays or Fridays, he shaves his remaining 36 Brahman Jajmans. He reserves Sundays for the Kyasth who is free on that day. The rest—one Bhat, one Kyasth, two Sunars, one Mali, two Kachhis, one Barhai, seven Kahars, one Gadariya, one Darzi, three Kumhars, two Mahajans, two Manihars and one Dhuna—are shaved when convenient for the barber. The Karimpur barber is helped by a fourteen year old son. He does not have a hair cutting parlor. He goes to his clients wherever they happen to be, resting or working, and performs his service. Shaving under the arms weekly, finger-nail cutting weekly, and toe-nail cutting fortnightly, are added to the tonsorial duties of the barber. Ordinarily hair is cut monthly except when his clients have their heads shaved for religious purposes or through choice. The residents of the village who are not the jajmans of our local barber use the services of a barber from Anjani, a village a mile away, or of another from Lahoripur, a village three-quarters of a mile away.

When a "kam-karnewala" comes into Karimpur from an outside village, he does not bear the same relationship to the community as a whole as does the "kam-karnewala" who has his residence in the village. But he may enjoy all the compensations and rights that exist between a jajman and a "kam-karnewala" in Karimpur. The bond between him and his jajman is as great as that between any other "kam-karnewala" and his jajman. But the "kam-karnewalas" of Karimpur lose by this relationship. Non-resident "kam-karnewalas" are generally not jajmans for Karimpur "kam-karnewalas". Their community jajmani relationships hold only where they reside, in so far as those services are adequate.

Both the barber and his wife are busy at the time of special ceremonies. He acts as a go-between in arrangements for weddings, and has thus become known as a match-maker. He is make-up man for the bridegrooms, sons of his jajmans, and his wife performs the same duties for the brides, daughters of their jajmans. He carrics gifts and sweets to the house of the bride. He distributes food to neighbours on special occasions. He collects milk and *ghee* (clarified butter) from neighbours when required for a special feast. At the time of a wedding he not only shaves the men in his own jajman's household, but he also shaves the guests from other villages—relatives of his jajmans. The Naiin, the wife of the barber, is kept busy in taking care of the women, especially the bride. She distributes sweets to the neighbours when they have been sent to her jajman's house by the groom at the time of the wedding and at other times. She oils the bodies of the women in her jajman's homes, shampoos their hair, and applies the henna colour to their feet and nails. When babies are born, she massages the mother and baby daily for a period of ten to fifteen days after the first ten days. She may be called upon to help in the preparation of food. There is no rest for the barber and his wife. They are among the few people in the village who devote their entire time to their jajmans. They have no time for farming.

Neither the local barber nor the outside barbers shave the Bhangi and Faqir. They will not serve these two groups because of objections which would be raised by the other jajmans.

10. THE KAHAR*. (*Water-Bearer*)

The Kahar, or water-bearer, is the chief among household menials. The presence of nineteen families

*Pronounced "Ka-hăr"

of Kahars in Karimpur is explained by the constant demands made by Brahmans for their help. They draw water daily for their high caste jajmans, and on special occasions for their lower caste jajmans—down through the Chamars. The women do most of the water carrying in the homes, whereas, the men do this work in the fields. The women assist in the grinding of grain, and cook and wash up the dishes for the bachelors in the community.

Eleven Kahar families average three to four Brahman jajmans per family except those whose services are monopolized by one or two of the most prosperous families. During the wedding season six to eight Kahars are required for carrying the heavy palanquin which conveys the groom to the bride's house for the wedding, or the bride to the groom's house on her first visit.

Most of the Kahar men are employed as day labourers in the fields. Some of the best among them are regularly employed. Others are more ambitious and cultivate their own fields. Those who are not prepared to supplement their jajmani rights, eke out a miserable existence. The women of this caste are the ones who perform most of the services. The boys help with cattle grazing. The opportunity for the men to serve as water-bearers comes chiefly when large groups of men are together, as at a wedding, or in the service of students, as at schools and colleges.

11. The Gadariya* (*Shepherd*)

The six Gadariya, or shepherd families, in Karimpur are gradually losing their identity. Three of the six had no sheep or goats in 1925 and only two had them in 1927. One family specialized on sheep and the other on goats. No other castes keep sheep, although a number of the

*Pronounced "Ga-dar-ee-yä"

menial castes keep goats, one or two to a family. The sheep are kept for wool and butchering. The goats are kept for milk and butchering. The shepherds milk, graze, cut wool and weave blankets. The butchering is done by another caste.

The Gadariyas, as shepherds, have very little opportunity to serve the villager. Most farmers keep their own milk animals, buffaloes, cows and goats, hence they do not need to get milk from the shepherd except on special occasions. The Gadariya with the goats finds a market for his milk in Mainpuri, five and a half miles away. There is very little demand for wool in the village. Most of the farmers grow their own cotton and are content with heavy homespun cotton blankets for the cold months. The woolen blankets do not have the same all year round utility and are difficult to stow away through the warm months, hence the Gadariya who has sheep, sells most of his wool to wandering buyers.

The majority of the Gadariyas, like other caste people in the village, engage in agriculture. Some have their own fields. Others work as day labourers. Those who keep herds do so no longer in the interests of the village, but for their own individual profit. They depend altogether on an outside market. They retain their grazing rights on the basis of custom. Many complaints are now heard against these men when they hack down branches from the evergreen trees to feed their animals, or when the animals trespass on growing fields. As the farmers improve their crops and take greater pride in their trees, the remaining Gadariyas may be obliged to engage in agriculture. The watching of the herds of buffalo and cattle is done by menials of the Kahar, Dhanuk and Chamar castes.

There are no representatives in Karimpur of the Ahir caste, which is the traditional cattle herding caste.

The Gadariyas of Karimpur utilize the services of the village although they themselves are given very little opportunity to serve others. Their income depends on what they realize from the sale of sheep and goats in outside markets and from what they may earn from their own fields or daily labour.

12. The Bharbhunja* (*Grain-Parcher*)

One family of Bharbhunjas do the grain parching for the village. Parched grain is very popular with the vegetarian Hindu. The Westerner is acquainted with puffed rice and popped corn. This is what the Hindu calls parched rice and parched maize. The Bharbhunja parches all cereals, in their season. At harvest time there is an abundance of grain to be parched and the Bharbhunjas are kept busy all day long. At other times of the year they can meet the demand by operating their furnace three evenings a week, except when there is a special ceremony or feast. They serve all castes in Karimpur and likewise serve the residents of nearby hamlets.

Parched or roasted gram (Cicer arietinum) which is used in the Indian army as emergency rations, is one of the most popular dry foods eaten by the villager. When he goes on a journey he generally has a supply of parched gram tied in a cloth bundle. It is often ground, mixed with water and drunk like oatmeal water. The women of the Bharbhunja family do the parching or roasting while the children gather the leaves and twigs that are used for fuel in the parching oven. Extra puffed rice is sometimes

*Pronounced "Bhár-bhoon-jä".

prepared from rice in store, and sold at the fairs or markets. The men of the family are engaged in agriculture to supplement the earnings from their traditional occupation, and the boys graze cattle.

13. The Darzi* (*Seamster*)

Five families of Darzis, or seamsters—in reality two households with divided eating arrangements—come next in the social scale of Karimpur. The work done by these men is of a very simple order. Several styles of shirts are made for men and boys. Jackets are made for women and girls. Some jajmans require vests and coats for the men and boys, and skirts for the women and girls. Cloth caps without visors, and quilts make up the remaining articles made for villagers. Other one-piece garments which require no cutting or fitting are simply seamed by hand or sewing machine. Styles never change and the Darzi has small demand made on his ingenuity.

One household with two *chulhas* (cooking places) has one male member. The other family has three brothers, each with his own cooking arrangements and each with a sewing machine. The majority of the prosperous jajmans are held by the senior of the three brothers. The other jajmans are divided among the remaining three Darzis, but are not fixed. The reason for this is that the Darzi who had this work, died. He had no son and his widow in an effort to keep the jajmani rights, called in her son-in-law. He did not have the same claim as a son would have had, and some of his father-in-law's jajmans are wavering between him and the brothers in the other family. The family of three brothers supplement their village earnings by doing work for other hamlets and by engaging

*Pronounced "Dér-zee".

in agriculture. They stand ready to serve all castes in the village and in return are served by all.

14. The Kumhar* (*Potter*)

Three families of Kumhars, potters, who rank next in the social scale, supply clay pots to the village. They gather the clay, shape the pots, bake and deliver them to their customers. Apart from special ceremonies for which clay vessels are required, their heaviest demand comes prior to the two big festival days when every village housewife requires fresh water jars. The Kumhar makes for village use, large round-bellied water jars, various types of jars used for milking, boiling, churning, etc., lids for water and milk jars, funnel-shaped tobacco pipe bowls, saucers which are used for the mustard oil lights, saucers for serving liquid foods at weddings, cups without handles, jars for storing grain, smaller jars for preserving spices and chutneys, feeding jars for cattle, and various other types of clay vessels.

Clay jars are handled carefully by thrifty village housewives and few are broken. Also, tin lamps are beginning to make their way into the village to replace the clay saucer-lights. Consequently, between the seasons of special demand, the potters have considerable spare time. This time they utilize by doing hauling work with their donkeys, which they must keep for carrying the clay from the river bed. They visit different hamlets and purchase dung fuel cakes. These they take into Mainpuri where they wander about through the streets seeking customers. There is always a demand for fuel and they are able to make a commission large enough to warrant their engaging in this activity.

---

*Pronounced "koom-här".

The three families although having separate eating arrangements—two families of four each and one family of one—represent one earning group, and together meet the requirements of the village and of hamlets nearby. The one Kumhar, who lives alone, limits his activities largely to the purchase and sale of fuel dung cakes.

15. MAHAJAN* (*Tradesman*)

The three Mahajan, or tradesmen families in the village rank next, not because of the inferiority of their work, but because of the social standing of those who have married into this group. Many so-called Mahajans are members of the Vaisya caste, the third of the division of Hindus. They are among the Twice-Born and have a high social standing. The local Mahajans would like to claim an equally high standing but their neighbours know too much about their forebears.

They all engage in trade and keep small shops from which one can purchase grain, spices, sugar and tobacco. They are not the only tradesmen in the village. Two Brahmans sell similar articles. The shop business done by these tradesmen is very small. The villagers usually make their few purchases in Mainpuri, but there are times when supplies run low or when credit is desired. Then the local shopkeeper is patronized. The most ambitious Mahajans do a certain amount of trade in grain for farmers who do not trouble to haul their goods to the market. They all supplement their earnings with agriculture.

Their claim to a share in the jajmani system is one of caste and residence. Their service which may at one time have been an essential one is not now essential,

---

*Pronounced "Má-häj-un".

because the farmers ordinarily market their own produce in nearby trading centres, and can make their neccesary purchases at the same centres. They patronize and are patronized by all the castes in Karimpur. Two of them have their shops by the main roadside and pick up enough extra outside trade to enable them to continue doing business in Karimpur.

16. The Teli* (*Oil Presser*)

The four families of Telis are the lowest of the Sudra castes living in Karimpur. They are engaged in the traditional work of oil-pressing. Oil plays an important part in village economy. It supplies a frying medium and shortening. It makes possible a dim light for household chores at night and is useful as an embrocation for aching joints. It is used as a lubricant for creaky cart-wheels and as a softener for leather waterbags. The various oils used for the above purposes are pressed from mustard, sesamum and castor seed. Occasionally neem (Melia Azadirachta) berries or mahua (Bassia Latifolia) flowers or poppy seeds are pressed.

Although the need for oil is constant, the greatest demands are made upon Telis at harvest time. They keep very little stock on hand because the patrons prefer the oil pressed from their own seed. But there is an occasional demand for oil. This oil is made from seed purchased in Mainpuri. The heavy part of the work is done by the women. The men scout around for business. The entire jajmani rights of the Telis are held by three families, representing three brothers. The fourth family is represented by a hunchback with a tubercular knee. He renders what service he can, to the three brothers. One brother has

*Pronounced "Téh-lee".

supplemented his earnings somewhat by prescribing herbs and powders for sick people. Another brother supplements his earnings by collecting the bark of the Babul (Acacia Arabica) tree which is used for tanning purposes. This he sells to traders in tanning bark. All of them engage in a small amount of agriculture. They are a sickly looking crowd and have very little ambition. They meet the requirements of their occupation in the village but attempt to do little more.

17. The Dhobi* (*Washerman*)

We come now to the group of outcastes. The one Dhobi, or washerman family in the village, is the highest among the outcastes in Karimpur. Dhobis are considered to be outcastes because they wash blood-stained clothes. However, their social standing does not affect their importance in the economic life of the village.

This family washes the clothing of 109 families. Two outside Dhobis wash for 44 families. None of the Dhobis will wash for the Bhangis, cesspool cleaners. The Dhobi is one of the few serving classes in Karimpur who has a full-time job. He, with the help of his wife and children, washes the clothes of prosperous villagers once every two weeks, of those less prosperous once a month, and those of the still less favoured, every six weeks or two months. Their work is as simple as it can be made. The clothes are called for, soaked over night, washed the next morning—weather permitting—dried on the ground and returned within twenty-four hours. They do no ironing. If they did, they would add considerably to their labour and get very little in return for it. The Laws of Manu say:

*Pronounced "Dhó-bee".

"A washerman shall wash (the clothes of his employers) gently on a smooth board of Salmaliwood; he shall not return the clothes (of one person) for those (of another), nor allow anybody (but the owner) to wear them. (Chap. VIII: 396)."

18. The Dhanuk* (*Mat Maker*)

The seven Dhanuk, or mat-making families, serve the community largely as agricultural labourers. They furnish their jajmans with a trumpet blower for festive occasions—it is he who announces the arrival of a wedding party—, and with a midwife when a baby is born. Date-palm leaf mat-making and fan-making are incidental services, since very few of the villagers feel the need for them. Two of the old men in the group who are not able to help in field work devote themselves to the more limited activities of mat and fan-making. A few jajmans such as Kachhis, Kahars and occasionally a Brahman request the Dhanuks to make leaf platters for their feasts.

In some village communities not far distant, the midwifery work is done by Bhangi women, but as far back as the present villagers' memories go, Dhanuk women have performed this service in Karimpur. The Dhanuks keep pigs and supply a village watchman. One other Dhanuk is frequently employed as a night watchman in Mainpuri, five and a half miles distant. Two of the men are full-time labourers for prosperous Brahmans. A few supplement their earnings from day labour, by cultivating their own small fields. The women supplement family earnings by grinding grain for their jajmans, and by watching ripening crops and fruit. The boys help by grazing cattle. By performing these various services they have succeeded in maintaining a much higher

*Pronounced "Dhän-uk".

standard than the menial group that is next lower to them, namely the Chamars.

19. THE CHAMAR* (*Leather Worker*)

The eight families of Chamars, or leather workers, most nearly approximate the position of slaves of any menial castes in the village. Their work with leather is but a small part of their life, as judged from the attitude of the average Brahman jajman. They skin the dead animals, sun dry, and sell them. They also put crude patches on the few slipper-like shoes that are found in the village. They reinforce the irrigation-baskets with leather and sew up the large leather bags that are used for drawing water for field irrigation. But most of the time they are at the beck and call of their jajmans.

> "In the village he is regarded not as an individual, but as So-and-So's Chamar. Outside of the intimate affairs of family life, his time and his services, and his son's time and services are in the hands of his master. His wife too must be ready to help in the fields or at the heavier tasks in the house of the patron, whenever sent for. The patron's work and interests come first. If there is any time left over, the Chamar and his sons spend it on the plot of land granted him as payment for his services. He makes no plans and undertakes nothing which involves time or money, without the consent of his patron" (Page 53, "Behind Mud Walls", C. V., and W. H. Wiser).

The Chamars are called upon to do all kinds of field work, from the hauling and spreading of manure, through every process, up to the carrying of the winnowed grain into the house. They are called upon to make sun-baked bricks, to build up broken mud walls, and to plaster the mud walls prior to the coming of the torrential rains. They are called upon to make baskets and ropes, to feed

*Pronounced "Chá-mär".

the cattle and to clean up the cattle rooms. They make and repair roofs, lay bricks, cut stone and dig wells. The women folk are expected to serve in the households to which the men are attached. When a Chamar plasters the outside of a house, his wife plasters the upper section of the inner-courtyard walls, the women of the house preferring to plaster the lower surfaces themselves. Chamar wives may help with the cleaning and grinding of grain, the husking of rice, the ginning of cotton, or with any other household tasks which workers so low are allowed to share. In the fields they cut sugarcane, sorghum, millet, and sometimes wheat, and they pick cotton.

The Chamars have some fields of their own but as has already been indicated they have very little time that they can call their own, and they cannot find many consecutive days to apply to their own fields. It is stated that for this reason some of the bolder spirits moved away from the village. Nesfield describes the position of the Chamar:

> "Originally he seems to have been an impressed labourer (begar) who was made to hold the plough for his master, and received in return a space to build his mud hut near the village, a fixed allowance of grain for every working day, the free use of wood and grass on the village lands, and the skins and bodies of animals that died. This is very much the status of the Chamar at the present day. He is still the field slave, the grass cutter, and the carrion-eater of the Indian village." (Crooke, op. cit. II, page 169.)

The Chamars average five Brahman jajmans per family, although several have only two or three Brahman jajmans. One family, a father with four sons has sixteen Brahman jajmans, giving each jajman an average of one-third of a Chamar. What usually happens is that the most powerful of the jajmans gets most of the Chamar's time and the others take what is left. The result is that

Kahars and Dhanuks have been worked into many jobs usually held by Chamars. The Chamars are, from the standpoint of the Brahman, most desirable because they are less independent. The Chamars have all other castes in the village as their jajmans as well. But apart from special leather work or help at a wedding, they have little time left for services of their humbler patrons. They are one group in the village who would be happy if they were less popular.

20. The Bhangi* (*Sweeper and Cesspool Cleaner*)

Lowest in the Karimpur Hindu scale of outcastes are the Bhangis, or sweepers and cleaners. They are still so rated by the people of Karimpur, although they have been baptized as Christians. They have changed their theology but still function as part of a Hindu system. Their responsibility to their jajmans sometimes involves them in Hindu religious ceremonies. Even if they were recognized as Christians and did not have a share in these religious ceremonies, their heredity, so well known to their neighbours, would give them the same social rating in Karimpur.

Their responsibility to their jajmans is that of cleaning cesspools and privies, and in sweeping the roads in front of the houses. The villagers do the sweeping within their own homes. There are only fourteen privies in the village—used by "purdah" women—but every house has a cesspool and a drain. Like so many of the menial services performed in the village, the heaviest part of the load falls on the women. They clean the privies daily, and the cesspools and drains once or twice a week. The sweeping in front

*Pronounced "Bhŭng-ee".

of houses which is done by the men, is done only on special feast days or at the time of ceremonies when there is a general clean-up in the jajman's house. To this is often added the sweeping of the threshing floor before the freshly harvested grain is brought in. The Bhangis go to their hamlet jajmans only twice a year—just often enough to keep their hold on the special claims that are theirs as Bhangis. Of course they would render the same service to hamlet jajmans at the time of a wedding.

The chief assistants of the Bhangis in their village scavenging work are their swine. Early every morning they are driven through the lanes of the village to clean up any filth that may have been deposited there during the night. The swine and their bristles form the largest source of cash income realized by the Bhangis.

The Bhangi men are also called upon by their jajmans to act as night watchmen when the jajmans are leaving the house overnight. They are frequently called upon to be messengers. Several of them supplement their earnings by weaving baskets. Others make feeble attempts at agriculture. The services rendered by them are so spasmodic that they find the close application required in agriculture, most irksome. One of the men is a village watchman. Others go off to the cities to work for Europeans while their wives, mothers and widowed sisters stay home to retain their jajmani.

Each family has a sufficiently large jajmani either in the village or in nearby hamlets to give them the subsidy they require for their simple standard of living. They, more than any other group in Karimpur, are familiar with what a city can offer in a larger cash income, but most of them prefer what the village grants them.

21. The Faqir* (*Mohammedan Beggar*)

The eight families of Faqirs, or traditional beggars, make up the highest of the four groups of Mohammedans in the village. It is most interesting to note that although these four groups are not followers of the Hindu religion, yet as residents of the village they have their jajmans. It might be explained in the cases of those who render particular services, but the right to beg seems a slimsy tie. The Faqirs do render one slight service which may account for their jajmani relationship—namely, that of beating the drum at the time of a wedding or other ceremony for which a jajman requires publicity. But this service is paid for at the time, and does not account for the privilege to beg. We find one family with fourteen Brahman jajmans, one Bhat, two Sunars, two Kachhis, one Lodha, four Barhais, one Nai, five Kahars, two Gadariyas, one Dhobi, one Dhanuk, two Chamars and two Manihars. Another Faqir family has twelve Brahman jajmans, one Mali, eleven Kachhis, four Barhais, four Kahars, two Gadariyas, one Bharbhunja, five Darzis, three Kumhars, one Mahajan, four Telis, three Dhanuks, six Chamars, and one Dhuna.

The other families have the remaining jajmans, and jajmans in nearby hamlets. But they make their living largely through agriculture or hiring out as agricultural labourers. There is therefore a limit to the number that the community is ready to recognize as hereditary beggars. And the members of these families have been forced to do what other families with insufficient incomes have been required to do, namely engage in agriculture.

One may ask how Mohammedans can become a part of the Hindu Jajmani system. Theoretically, they

*Pronounced "Fa-kēer".

cannot, but practically, we find them in this year, 1932, members of the system. Several explanations may be given. They may originally have been Hindus and a part of the jajmani system. During the period of Mohammedan rule they may have become Mohammedans, and under the protection of Mohammedan rulers, retained their old village rights to land and service. They may have been settled in the village by the Mohammedan rulers whose interests they protected. They may have settled in the village and won the favour of the village headmen, who established them in their present position. We have described in "Behind Mud Walls" (pages 41-42) how "they have made themselves as much Hindu and as little Mohammedan as possible." Whatever the causes may have been, the Mohammedans of Karimpur occupy, in some respects, a position better than that of the Dhobi, Dhanuk, Chamar, and Bhangi, in that Brahmans will share their pipes with them.

22. The Manihar* (*Mohammedan Bangle Seller*)

The two families of Manihars, bangle sellers, are the next in the social order of Mohammedans living in Karimpur. They do not depend on Karimpur alone for their earnings. They have divided the surrounding area into two sections which they cover over a given period. They usually go no further than a round distance which can be covered within a day. Occasionally they stay away over night. Their margin of profit is small, hence they have to keep moving. They sell their wares at the various religious fairs. All women and girls (except widows) wear at least two pairs and usually four to six, of coloured bangles. Sales are aided by custom. The Manihar supplies each bride

*Pronounced "Manee-hár"

with seven pairs of lac bracelets. Also, when a baby arrives, the mother breaks her glass bracelets. And then, at the time of the purification ceremony the Manihar is called in to fit on new ones. Unmarried daughters of Brahman, Bhat, Kyasth, Sunar, Kahar, Gadariya and Bharbhunja jajmans are given a pair of bracelets free each year.

The Manihars depend on the services of Karimpur residents except in matters of religious ceremonies. At that time they have to call in their own Mohammedan helpers. This however does not interfere with most of the services rendered in Karimpur.

23. The Dhuna* (*Mohammedan Cotton Carder*)

The one Dhuna family cards practically all of the cotton used within the village. The cotton carder not only cards the cotton but fills quilts and jackets, makes the "fingers" ready for the housewives to spin into threads, and rolls wicks for the small saucer lamps. The busy season is during the cold months, December and January, when the cotton is freshly picked and quilts are in demand. After this the work rapidly decreases until the carders have very little to card by the first of March. Like the other workers in the village who have to depend on seasonal demands, they are engaged in agriculture, both for themselves and for others.

They serve all who come to them, many in the course of a good cotton season, or few in the course of a poor season. They keep a little cotton in stock for those who may require it. The Dhunas depend almost entirely on the farmers to supply their own cotton. Like the Manihar they are jajmans for most of the services in Karimpur,

---

*Pronounced "Dhoon-ä"

hence form an intrinsic part of the Hindu Jajmani system there.

24. The Tawaif* (*Mohammedan Dancing Girl*)

The two families of Tawaifs, Mohammedan dancing girls, comprise two elderly women, only one of whom is able to serve the community, and she, not very effectively. She is subject to call by any of the villagers who want her songs at a festive occasion.

These women were brought into the village by a prosperous Kyasth more than fifty years ago. They were the mistresses of several of the prosperous men and were available as dancing girls, at weddings or entertainments. They have served as dancing girls ever since, but the calls have become fewer year by year. They supplement their meagre earnings by spinning cotton and selling goats. They are not permitted to starve, however, as they can always receive alms. The youngest of the two is one of the handsomest and best preserved of the older women in the village. They make few demands on the services of other villagers and in turn they have little opportunity to render service, but they are free to call on the families of their old jajmans at any time for help.

25. Non-Resident Services

Three services essential to the self-sufficiency of Karimpur are lacking, namely those of the weaver; brass, copper and bell metal worker; and astrologer. The first and last come to the village. The second is patronized in shops at Mainpuri or at religious fairs. Many other services are utilized, however. The villagers patronize from time to time sweetmeat sellers, fruit vendors, leaf-

---

*Pronounced "Ta-whý-if"

plate makers, sellers of the betel leaf and areca nut for chewing, shoe makers, calico printers, cloth merchants, notions vendors, braid and silk fringe makers, the dyers of cloth, sheet-iron box makers, tin smiths, kiln brick makers, wandering cattle merchants, grain merchants, perfumers, red lead and forehead spangle makers, medicine vendors, book-sellers, ink makers, cutlers, lock makers, toy, kite and bird-cage makers, priests and maulvis (Mohammedan religious leaders), religious mendicants, conjurors, snake charmers, exhibitors of trained animals, tumblers and acrobats, firework makers, and dancing girls.

No jajmani relationship is established with any of these outsiders. It is the custom of families generally to patronize the same tradesman but there is no hard and fast rule. It would be possible, however, for families from any of these groups to move into the village and in course of time establish a jajmani relationship. Residence in a village together with a desire to establish the relationship are requisite for membership in the jajmani system. Articles such as bicycles, sewing machines, and sugarcane pressess are now being purchased in the village. As the demand for these articles is so limited, merchants selling them could not establish a relationship on a symmetrical level.

SECTION II

Jajmani Compensation and Rights in Karimpur

TO counterbalance the functional responsibilities of the "kam karne-walas" (those who serve) as listed in Section I, the "kam karne-walas" have equally important compensations and rights. These are realizable in exchange for services rendered. The means by which these compensations and rights are realized, differ. They may be realized in the form of service, cash or kind payment, in a variety of concessions or a combination of the three. These compensations and rights are maintained according to custom, which is supported by the village elders, the sacred books of the Hindus and the Law of the State. No generalization can be made as to these compensations and rights, because each occupational group has acquired its own individual status. No attempt has been made to equalize them, and no one dares to criticize the status of another. The jajmani status of each group is inherent in its occupational function, which is governed by birth and established by custom.

I. Means of Realization

A. Services:

The barber, grain parcher, potter and washerman exchange services. Their interrelationship is the most symmetrical relationship in the village. They each value the services of the other equally. They serve each other as they would serve other castes in the village, and expect no supplementary payments. They occupy approximately the same economic status and can render no additional services to each other. This interrelationship of service extends to no other castes, because no others can render an equality of service. Their demands upon each other are fairly constant whereas those upon other services are not so constant.

One carpenter, Nek Ram, does the ordinary carpentry work for the two bard families and for one Mohammedan beggar family, free of charge. There is in this case an exchange of services but it is on an asymmetrical level. The carpenter does more for the bards and beggar than they do for him. The Mohammedan beggars get occasional gifts in the form of services from other occupational groups as well, such as a few clay jars from the potter, a bit of oil from the oil presser, some parched grain from the grain parcher, etc., etc., but this cannot be considered in the same class as the interrelationship existing among the barber, grain parcher, potter and washerman.

B. Fixed Payment:

The daily, monthly, bi-yearly, piece-rate and special occasion payments represent the fixed cash and kind payments made in the village. They cannot be compared with payments made for similar kinds of work outside of the jajmani system. They are not sufficient in themselves. They are in addition to certain concessions which will be discussed further on. The jajman when he makes a cash payment thinks not in terms of value for value received, but that the payments together with certain concessions will give the "kam karne-wala" his livelihood. To determine the exact economic status of a given occupation is therefore complicated. These fixed rates show little sign of changing throughout the course of years. They have been fixed by custom and will not change until the custom changes, although a slight alteration is made from time to time in daily and monthly payments, based on the buying power in terms of grain.

1. *Daily:*

The prosperous farmers in the village give frequent employment by the day to men in 2 Kachhi, 3 Kahar, 2 Gadariya, 2 Dhanuk, 4 Chamar and 1 Faqir family—14 out of 161 families in the village. In addition men in 10 Kachhi, 6 Barhai, 13 Kahar, 1 Gadariya, 3 Dhanuk, 4 Chamar, 1 Bhangi, 5 Faqir and 1 Dhuna families are prepared from time to time to work by the day as labourers in agricultural work or building repairs. The calls to work come chiefly from the jajmans, or if made by others, are made with the consent of the jajman who always has first call on his "kam karnewalas". One Kahar for whose work we kept a daily work schedule showed that he alternated in his daily work among about a dozen Brahmans, serving his own jajmans in the main and the others when he was free. His daily payment was 2 *Chapatis* *and 4 annas (8 cents). Other "kam karnewalas" serve their jajmans daily but for a limited period of time. This will be described under piece-work. Carpenters receive 8 annas (.16) and two meals when they work at a jajman's house. When they go to a neighbouring village, they charge 10-12 annas (.20-.24) plus food.

2. *Monthly:*

Three of the most prosperous farmers in the village each employ a labourer by the month. The men thus employed are an Ahir from a neighbouring village, a

*Chapatis—unleavened bread.

Gadariya and a Dhanuk from Karimpur. The maximum pay received by these men is 5 Rupees, 10 annas ($ 1.80) per month plus a noontime meal. They are called upon to do all kinds of tasks and are at work from 6 a.m., when they start chopping fodder for the animals, until 8-9 p.m., when they finish up their chores. This form of service is not as popular with the "kam karnewalas" as the daily labour. There is a smaller cash income and less freedom for the "kam karnewalas." In every instance where the men are giving full-time service they are in debt to their jajmans and paying off the debt through service.

A monthly rate is paid to the boys, and in two cases to men, for herding the village cattle. They are paid at the rate of 4 annas (.08) for a buffalo, 2 annas (.04) for a cow, and 1 anna (.02) for young stock per head per month. In no case does the herdsman's income exceed 4 Rupees ($ 1.28) per month. Several villagers, 2 Brahmans, and 1 Bhangi, serving as messengers for the two landlords, and 1 Dhanuk and 1 Bhangi serving as watchmen for the Government police are likewise on a monthly salary, earning 8 Rupees*; 8 Rupees; 4 Rupees; 2 Rupees, 14 annas; and 2 Rupees, 14 annas per month respectively, but this arrangement is outside of the jajmani system, as they draw their salaries from sources outside of the village.

3. *Bi-yearly:*

When the crops are harvested in the autumn and in the spring, all "kam karnewalas" are given grain. The less favoured ones have to go to the newly cut fields to get their "hand-out" of unthreshed grain. The more favoured

*NOTE: Dollar equivalents of Rupees will not be given hereafter. One anna equals roughly 2 cents; 16 annas make a Rupee which equals 32 cents; 4 pice equals 1 anna.

castes get their allotment of grain at the house, after it has been threshed and winnowed.

The less favoured castes represent the bulk of the "kam karnewalas" and include all excepting the carpenter, iron–worker, barber, water-bearer, potter and washerman. These too in some cases have to take their grain in unthreshed form. A jajman gives to his "kam karnewala" from only one field. If he has a number of different crops the "kam karnewala" has to choose which kind of grain he may prefer. And the "kam karnewala" has to be on hand when the cut crops are being bundled to be carried to the threshing floor. Because of this custom the "kam karnewala" has to cover quite a bit of territory at the close of each day during the harvesting season.

The carpenter, iron-worker, barber, water-bearer, potter and washerman have fixed allotments. The Brahman jajmans give the carpenter and iron-worker $10\frac{1}{2}$ pounds of grain each season per plough owned, whereas all of the non-Brahman jajmans give 14 pounds of grain each season per plough owned. The barber is given 7 pounds of barley and 14 pounds of wheat at spring harvest and 7-$10\frac{1}{2}$ pounds of corn on the cob, one head load of sorghum yielding 7 pounds of grain plus fodder, and 7 pounds of unhusked rice at autumn harvest. The latter two are received only if the barber goes to his jajman's field. From non-cultivators he receives 10 pounds of grain per head per year. The water-bearer receives from his Brahman and Kyasth jajmans 8.4 pounds of grain each season. The potter receives the same as the barber. The washerman receives what the carpenter gets from one plough. He gets an additional handful of from 1 to 1 2/5 pounds of grain if he is present at the threshing floor ceremony just before the freshly winnowed grain is weighed up. The owner of the pile does obeisance to the broom and the winnowing basket and requests the gods that the total weight may be large. He then takes out the *Dhobi ki ujari* (offering to the local gods) and puts it to one side. The faithful Hindu never fails to do this. Others may have to be reminded by the Dhobi (washerman). Some altogether ignore the custom.

The other castes receive in the nature of a charity "hand-out" 1.4—2.8 pounds of unthreshed grain if they present themselves in the field when the stalks are being bundled to be taken to the threshing floor. No one who comes to a jajman's field is turned down unless the recipient has had a share from another field of his in that season. The good Hindu is taught that he receives merit by giving grain to those who request it. The amounts given are not large but make a helpful addition to the family granary if some member of the family can get to the different jajmans at the appointed time. If the season is a good one the jajman may be more generous and give up to 5 or 7 pounds of grain. The grains which he gives in the smallest amounts are the lentils. The Kachhis give a head of cauliflower and a few sweet potatoes to their "kam karnewalas" if they come to the fields at the time of harvest. When sugarcane is first cut each "kam karnewala" gets 3 or 4 stalks in the field. Later when the sugarcane is pressed they are given 2.8 to 3.5 pounds of sugarcane juice.

4. *Per piece of work*:

The daily income of the majority of castes in Karimpur is made up of cash and kind payments made by the jajmans in exchange for specific services rendered. The goldsmith receives 2 pice per tola (175 grains) for making solid ornaments of silver, 2 annas per tola for making filigree ornaments of silver, 6 annas per tola for making solid ornaments of gold and 2 Rupees, eight annas per tola for making filigree ornaments of gold. The vegetable grower receives the market price for his vegetables, melons and tobacco. The carpenter makes small articles such as small wooden platters, bread boards, spuds and sickles, costing 2 annas to 6 annas up to ox-carts costing from 20 Rupees to 85 Rupees, the carpenter in each case supplying the materials. Brahmans pay the Gadariyas 1 anna per quart for goat's milk. Non-Brahmans pay $1\frac{1}{2}$ annas per quart. The water-bearer is given daily one *chapati* weighing about .35 pounds at each one of the houses to which he carries water. He gets 3.5 pounds of grain when he carries water to the field workers. The grain parcher receives from non-Brahmans 16 2/3 per cent of the total amount of grain given to him to parch and 8 1/3 per cent from Brahmans. Where cash is paid, he is given 1 anna for parching 7 pounds of grain. When rice is puffed, the grain parcher has to give his jajman puffed rice weighing 1/3 the total weight of rice given to him. The grain parcher realizes the difference, if there is any. The seamster receives from 2 to 12 annas for making various articles of clothing for non-Brahmans, and one half that amount when working for Brahmans. These payments are usually made in grain. The jajman supplies the cloth and thread. The potter is paid by the piece or by the hundred in the case of small articles for all things made by him in addition to the 18 narrow-mouthed water vessels, and the 6 vessels used in food preparation which must be supplied to each jajman three times a year. The prices range from 2 annas per hundred in the case of small clay saucers to 10 annas per hundred for large saucers. The largest pieces made by them are large water vessels or vessels for storing grain. They range in price from 4 to 12 annas. The oil presser gives 1/3 mustard oil, 2/5 sesamum oil, and 1/4 castor oil in exchange for any quantity of oil seed given to him for pressing. Any balance, together with the crushed seed, is his for the service. The washerman is given a *chapati* weighing about .35 pounds each time he delivers a wash. The Dhanuk is paid 6 annas for a strip of matting 1½ yards wide by 3 to 4 yards long, and 1 pice to 1 anna for a fan. The leather workers get 7 pounds of grain for making a new leather well bucket, 2 annas or less for repairing the leather well bucket and a *chapati* or less than that for repairing shoes. They sell baskets for from 2 pice to 2½ annas. The wife of the cesspool cleaner is given a *chapati* similar to the one given to the water-bearer and washerman every time she cleans the household cesspool or privy. Two of the Mohammedan beggars get about .175 pounds of grain every two weeks from the different households. They give no service in exchange. The Mohammedan bangle seller receives 1 pice for from one to six bracelets depending on the quality. For cheap metal jewelry he receives from 12 annas to 1 Rupee, 6 annas, per pound. The cotton carder receives a quantity of grain equal in weight to the amount of cotton he is asked to card. These rates may seem a bit complicated to an outsider but are known to every man, woman and child in the village.

5. *Special Occasions*:

The special occasions afford great inducements to all "kam karnewalas". It is to these times that they look for additional payments in cash and kind. It gives every one a forward look. The jajman can always get an extra job or two done on the strength of impending festivities. There is a certain glamour about the payments made on these special occasions not found in the humdrum daily, monthly, bi-yearly and piece work payments. The "kam karnewalas" have partaken in many such occasions before and know almost exactly what they will receive. But there will be delicacies not tasted for a long time, and there is always the general air of festivity. Their behaviour is very much like that of western boys just before Christmas.

Of these special occasions the wedding is the most important. In most instances individuals are in reality paid only what they have earned in doing the extra tasks assigned to them. But whatever is given is regarded not as a matter of payment but as a matter of pleasure. The amounts which the various castes may earn in a marriage are listed below. It must be remembered that the amount given always depends on the means of the jajman. The amounts given below represent the average given in Karimpur. More may be given at times. Often, less is given. Furthermore the services of the castes listed below are not used by all. Brahmans and others who stand high in the community are expected to use the services of all castes.

The Brahman priest serves from 2 to 4 days. He gives all of his time if it is the wedding of a son, as the wedding party goes to the home of the bride. He receives from 5 to 25 Rupees.

The bard serves as a messenger and recites some verses. He gives from 2 to 6 days and receives from 2 to 4 Rupees.

The goldsmith gets the value of his handwork as contracted, and is suspected of having methods of reducing the amount of pure metal, gold or silver, which is supplied to him, according to the ability of the purchaser to detect the substitution. The value of the gold or silver used varies from 50 Rupees to 400 Rupees.

The florist furnishes the head-dress and necklace of flowers for which he receives from 8 annas to 1 Rupee. For other flowers and henna supplied he gets 8 annas.

The vegetable grower has the privilege of presenting a visiting wedding party with a basket of vegetables in the hope of receiving special remuneration.

The carpenter receives from 2 Rupees, 8 annas to 5 Rupees for a girl's wedding when he furnishes a *charpai** and 1 Rupee for a low platform 2 feet square. He receives no special pay for his labour in cutting fuel for the preparation of the food for the guests. For a boy's wedding he supplies sandals for which he receives from 8 annas to 1 Rupee.

The barber and his wife serve off and on for 15 days for which one or the other receives 1 Rupee—at the *Pili Chitthi* (for carrying the letter announcing the date of the marriage), 1 Rupee at the *Lagan* (for carrying the letter announcing the complete programme of the wedding ceremonies), 1 Rupee at the *Nikrausi* (when the bridegroom leaves his home), 1 Rupee at *Darwaza* (the arrival of the bridegroom at the bride's home), 1 Rupee at *Bhanvaren* (the circumambulation of the bride and bridegroom round the sacred fire), 1 Rupee at the *Bida* (when the bride leaves her father's home), 1 Rupee at the *Ganth Jurai* (the ceremony of knotting together the clothes of the bride and bridegroom), and about 1 Rupee in small amounts at various times throughout the ceremonies. When weddings do not come frequently in the household of a jajman, the barber's wife receives in addition a new skirt and scarf, at a son's wedding.

---

*Charpai—a roped cot.

The water-bearer and his wife serve for about 15 days for which one or the other receives at the *Lagan* (see barber), 1 Rupee, at the *Kals* (for carrying water to the door upon the arrival of the bridegroom's party) 1 Rupee, at the *Sherbet* (for supplying sweetened water to the bride and groom and other important guests) 1 Rupee, at the *Panware* in the case of a daughter's wedding (for supplying water to the visiting wedding party) 1 Rupee, at the *Bhanvaren* (see barber) 1 Rupee, at the *Bida* (see barber) 1 Rupee, and at the *Bidai* (an extra *Bida* gift) 1 Rupee, and in the case of the wedding of a son, when the bridegroom returns to his home 1 Rupee. The wife of the water-bearer like the wife of the barber receives a skirt and scarf at a son's wedding. The water-bearer family which owns the palanquin in which the bride or groom is carried gets 1 Rupee rental for its use. The six or eight water-bearers who carry the palanquin receive 1 Rupee or 1½ Rupees each.

The shepherd furnishes a wristlet made of wool for the bridegroom for which he receives from 2 annas to 1 Rupee.

The grain parcher receives a total of from 2 to 6 annas in small amounts at various times during the wedding ceremony. He is paid at the regular rate by non-Brahmans and less by Brahmans for parching grain that may be required, and for grinding tobacco. The wife of the grain parcher is given either a skirt or scarf, more generally the latter.

The seamster receives 1 Rupee for from 2 to 4 days work on the clothes of the bride and regular fees for clothes made for other members of the family. In a daughter's marriage he receives 1 Rupee for presenting a fan made of cloth, to the bridegroom.

The potter makes all the clay vessels necessary for the wedding in return for which he realizes from 3 Rupees to 4 Rupees on a daughter's wedding and from 1 Rupee to 2 Rupees on a son's wedding. The wife of the potter receives a skirt and scarf the same as the wife of the barber.

The tradesman has an opportunity of supplying spices for the wedding only in case enough were not purchased from the Mainpuri bazaar.

The oil presser furnishes mustard oil and receives the regular rate.

The washerman washes dirty clothes for the guests and receives 1 Rupee at *Mang Bharai* (when red colour is placed in the part of the bride's hair just before she leaves for her husband's home) and 1 Rupee at the time of *Bida* (see barber). The wife of the washerman receives a new skirt and scarf the same as the wife of the barber.

The mat maker supplies the leaf platters from which the guests eat, and occasionally a mat and fan. He receives nothing. His wife who helps in the household work is given a scarf at a son's wedding. The mat maker who blows the brass conch receives 1 Rupee.

(NOTES:—In some families, the leaf platters are taken from the Bari caste, who live in Mainpuri.)

The leather worker plasters the front doorway with cow-dung, digs the fireplace for the preparation of the food and makes baskets. He receives 2 Rupees at a daughter's marriage and 1 Rupee at a son's. The wife of the leather worker receives a scarf at a son's wedding.

The sweeper acts as night watchman when the wedding party is absent in another village and attends to all the sweeping necessary when a wedding party is in the village. He is given an old coat or shirt and his wife is given an old skirt and a new scarf. Where there is a privy in the house, the new bride on her first trip there, leaves a brass bowl or tumbler for the sweeper's wife. All the bits of food left over on the leaf platters are gathered up by the sweepers and taken to their homes. They collect from 7 to 28 pounds of left overs which are dried and stored for future use.

The Mohammedans in the village also have a share. The Faqir beats the drum and is given 1 to 2 Rupees. The bangle-seller presents all the woman in the household who have husbands, with glass bracelets. He receives for his wife a skirt and head scarf, or 1 to 2 Rupees. The cotton carder whips up the cotton for the quilt on which the bride or groom sits when riding in the palanquin. He receives grain in weight equal to the cotton and cloth used in the quilt. The dancing girl sings songs for which she receives 4 or 8 annas at a son's wedding and from 8 annas to 1 Rupee at a daughter's marriage.

At the time of a wedding, all the above participants are fed either part or all of the time. When the big feasts are held the employees bring their families who are also fed.

The next most important event in the life of the village employee is the death of a member of the jajman's family. With it are associated three occasions on which all have a feast, namely on the *Shuddh* or 10th day after death, the *Terhain* or 13th day after death and the *Barsi*, or during the 12th month after death. On the 10th day guests are fed rice and curry. On the 13th day and at the end of the year they are fed *puris**, *kachoris*†, curds and

*Puris—unleavened bread fried in deep fat.

†Kachoris—small unleavened bread fried in deep fat.

vegetables. In connection with the ceremonies attached to these days the Brahman priest receives from 2 Rupees to 10 Rupees and on the 13th day he is given a brass platter, brass bowl, pair of shoes, shirt, dhoti small white hat and umbrella. Twelve other Brahmans are given brass tumblers or *lotas** and a pice or a rupee each on the 13th day. The florist furnishes flowers on the 13th day; the carpenter cuts fuel for the funeral pyre; the barber carries the lighted bit of cow-dung fuel, some straw and a jar of water to the burning grounds, shaves the mourners and assists in the other duties which are assigned to him on feast days; the water-bearer carries water; the seamster sews the cloth used for a deceased woman; and the washerman washes the clothes of the deceased for all castes except sweepers. These services are performed without payment, unless the feasts are considered to be a type of payment. The sweeper gets the one strip of cloth about four yards in length which is thrown over the corpse as it is taken to the burning grounds. White cloth is used for men and red cloth for women. When the sweeper or the mat maker, or in special cases the bard or barber, carries the news of the death to relatives, he is given food for the journey at the rate of four *chapatis* and a few greens each day. The sweeper gets all the left over food from the three feasts.

Births, although very important occasions, are not of much value to the village "kam karnewalas" as a whole. The priest who prepares the child's horoscope and pronounces the mother clean, receives from 4 to 5 Rupees for his contribution. The goldsmith sometimes has the privilege of making ornaments for the new child. The florist

*Lotas—brass bowls.

supplies the flowers for the ceremony of *Mul Shant,** the date of which is fixed by the priest if the child is born under the 19th lunar asterism Scorpio. He also supplies flowers for the *Chhati* (the sixth day when the mother is allowed to leave the room in which the child is born) ceremony which occurs on the sixth day after birth. He receives 4 to 8 annas or grain. The wives of the water-bearer, barber and matmaker who have been assisting the family, have rights to share the grain which is used in various ceremonies. Their total individual shares may in this way amount to as much as 4 pounds. In addition the wives of the barber, water-bearer and matmaker receive a skirt and scarf when a son is born. The seamster sews a shirt and cap for the baby and receives 3 or 4 pounds of grain. The potter furnishes one clay jar and receives up to three pounds of grain. His wife is given a scarf. The oil presser may present oil in the hope of getting something extra such as grain and a scarf. The matmaker's wife who does the work of the midwife receives her wages. The sweeper is given 7 pounds of grain for a girl and 10 pounds of grain for a boy for removing the soiled clothes and after-birth. The Faqir may be asked to beat the drum on both the birthday and 6th day after birth in case a male child is born. For this service he may receive from 4 annas to 1 Rupee or its equivalent in grain. The bangleseller furnishes new glass bracelets for the mother of the new child on the 6th day and receives the price of the bracelets plus 2 to 8 annas additional. The dancing girl sings and

*Mul Shant—ceremony for appeasing the deity presiding over the 19th lunar asterism Scorpio.

(NOTE :—If it has been discovered in a family that it is inauspicious to hold the *Chhati* on the 6th day, it may be held 6 months after birth, or 6 years after birth).

receives a skirt and scarf, or money, ranging from 1 anna to 1 Rupee.

The first hair-cutting ceremony is the special privilege of the barber. At this time he receives from 1 anna to 1 Rupee together with a used skirt and scarf for his wife, and a shirt or a brass bowl or tumbler. Less is given for girls than for boys.

The biggest event in the life of a Twice-Born boy, next to the wedding, is that of the investiture of the sacred thread. There is a special feast at which all the "kam karnewalas" and their families are invited. In addition there are certain amounts paid out. The Brahman priest receives from 1 Rupee to 4 Rupees. The bard who takes invitations for which he gets road expenses, and who recites verses during the ceremony receives 1 Rupee. The florist who supplies mango leaves, flowers, and the fuel for the sacred fire receives from 1 to 12 annas. The carpenter who presents the youth with a pair of sandals and cuts the fuel for the food is given 1 Rupee. The barber who paints the edges of the boy's feet and gives an oil rub to the boy receives from 1 to 2 Rupees. The wife of the barber also helps without special remuneration. The 1½ to 3 pounds of grain used in the worship is the right of the barber. The water-bearer fills a jar with water and always receives 1 Rupee as his special right. He receives from 1 to 8 annas extra for other work done by himself and wife. The shepherd makes the woolen bracelet and receives from 4 to 8 annas. The grain parcher gets 2 to 4 annas although he has no special work. The potter gets from 1 to 1½ Rupees for supplying several large clay jars and the small clay individual cups used by the guests for drinking water. The washerman washes the clothes of the youth and gets from

2 to 4 annas. The matmaker supplies the leaf platters from which the guests eat and gets from 2 to 4 annas. The leather worker plasters the front doorway with cow-dung, for which he receives from 1 to 2 annas. The sweeper gets the left over food which amounts to from 7 pounds to 31 pounds. The bangleseller furnishes glass bracelets to all the women of the household and receives from 1 Rupee to 1½ Rupees.

Among the special occasions which depend on the will of the householder is the *Khatta* (singing of the religious poem "*Sat Narain Khatta*") which occurs in some houses every second year and in others every third, or fourth year. There is no regular time set. It is a matter of finances and religious zeal. A feast of *puris*, *kachhori*, curds, and vegetables is fed to the guests and all of the employees. The feast is the chief asset to the "kam karnewalas". The extras are very small, although the services performed are similar to those of other ceremonies. The Brahman receives 2 Rupees or more. In a recent *Khatta* the priest was given the use of several *bighas** of land rent free for one year, the value of which was not less than 10 Rupees. The water-bearer receives from 2 to 4 pice; the barber from 2 to 4 pice; the florist from 2 to 4 pice. (On this occasion he makes a special finger ring of *Dab* [Eragrostis cynosuroides] grass for the host); the potter from 2 to 4 pice; the bard from 2 to 4 pice for fastening a cotton bracelet on the jajman's wrist; the matmaker from 2 to 4 pice; and the sweeper, the left over food. The carpenter and leather worker perform their customary services but get no reward other than the privilege of eating at the feast.

*Bigha—.20 of an acre in Karimpur.

Birthdays are frequently observed by what is known as *Sui ki Puja** or *Jitariya puja*†. On the day of birth one ear of the child is pierced by a needle and a black thread inserted in the ear. In families where children have been dying or where mothers are fearful lest they might die, this needle is carefully kept and worshipped monthly on the day of the month on which the child is born, until a year has elapsed. After a year, the worship is kept up annually on birthdays until the time of the thread ceremony in the case of the Twice-Born or the time of marriage in the case of lower castes. The *Jitariya puja* is similar in that mothers observe the worship with the same goal of saving their children. In this case the god *Jitiya bart* (See Forbes Dictionary) is worshipped. The barber's wife and the mat-maker's wife divide the *Neochhavar* (presents passed three times around the head of the one for whom the worship is performed, and then given to menials in order to avert the evil eye). When divided, each share amounts to a few pice, and 6 to 12 ounces of grain. *Puris*, and 8 to 10 *batasas*‡ each are distributed to the friends and employees.

From time to time various deities are worshipped. At such times, the officiating priests and a few menials generally receive some small payments and all "kam karnewalas" receive some food. Data recorded for several such *pujas*§, show (1) in the case of a carpenter: the guests and workers were fed 28 pounds of *puris* (cooked with 5 pounds of *ghee*||) and 14 pounds of Indian Yam

*Sui ki puja—worship of the needle.

†Jitariya puja—worship of the god Jitiya bart.

‡Batasa—small sugar puffs.

§Puja—worship.

||Ghee—clarified butter.

(Coloeasia Antiquarum). The priest was given 2 pice *Dakshina* (money given to a Brahman after a feast) and the *Bhagat** 1 pound of maize. (2) In the case of a vegetable grower: the guests and workers were fed 70 pounds of *puris* (cooked in 1/5 its weight of *ghee*), 14 pounds of curds and 42 pounds of *Ghuniya* (Indian Yam). The priest was given 2 pounds of maize, and 4 annas for *Havan*†. The florist, barber and water-bearer were given 2 pice each. (3) In the case of a seamster: seventy men and twenty women were fed 82 pounds of *puris* (14 pounds of *ghee* being used), 40 pounds of Indian Yams, 10 pounds of brown sugar and 30 pounds of curds. 82 pounds of *Chapatis* were eaten by the women who lived in the household for a week and who helped to prepare the food for the feast. The *Jogi* (ascetic priest) took the money offered on the *Arti*. The *Arti* is a tray bearing in the centre a saucer made of wheat flour, filled with *ghee*. A small cotton wick lies in the *ghee*, and is lighted to make the lamp, used in worship. Around it the money is scattered. In this case there were a pice or two from each of the guests. The priest also received the one Rupee and five pice pasted on the cloth on which the Swastika was drawn, a waistcoat, cloth hat, shirt, and a woman's half jacket, and 2½ pounds wheat flour, 1 pound bottle gourds and 1 pound *ghee* for his return journey.

Apart from the irregular celebrations that depend on the ceremonial activities of the household, and which contribute considerably to the income of some of the menial classes, there are the regular religious bathing and feast days. The chief feature for the serving groups of some of these special days is the food. On certain days such as

*Bhagat—an exorcist, and a devotee of some goddess.
†Havan—burnt offering.

*Raksha Bandhan**, *Karwa Chauth*†, *Diwali*‡ and *Holi*§ the Brahman, Bhat, Kyasth, Sunar, Kachhi, Lodha, Barhai, Nai, Kahar, Gadariya and Teli jajmans give food to their "kam karnewalas". The Dhanuks and Bhangis are said to be the only ones who will take food from the Darzi jajmans. The Chamars claim that the Karimpur Darzis are descendants of a low sub-caste of Chamars hence they will not accept cooked food from Darzis. On other holidays the Brahman priests are generally the favoured ones. The Hindu calendar of religious dates recognized in Karimpur is herewith given and those dates noted which are of any economic value to the serving groups.

Four dates in each month, new moon, full moon, and the eleventh day of each half month, are observed by certain persons without fail. Following the death of a Brahman, a pundit is fed on each *Amawas* (New Moon) until a year has elapsed. Faithful Hindus perform religious ceremonies on every *Puranmashi* (full moon). The florist always supplies the faithful with a small garland for which he is given two *puris* on the following day. At the time of the worship two *tikki* (little *puris*) and two *batasas* are given to each of the children who come for them. The priest is fed by the faithful on four or five *Puranmashis* in the year. The 11th (*ekadasi*) of each half month is observed as a fast day by a widow until a year has elapsed after the death of her husband. On each day following the fast a priest is fed. (The *Puranmashi* worship is not carried on in households for a year where there have been deaths in the

---

*Raksha Bandhan—the ceremony of wearing a wrist amulet.

†Karwa Chauth—fast day of women with object of bringing prosperity on their husbands and sons.

‡Diwali—the feast of lamps.

§Holi—the spring feast or carnival.

family). In the following calendar, these dates will be omitted unless they have additional significance.

April 3—17, 1927*. *Chait* (Light Half) (From day after New Moon through Full Moon).

April 3—11. 1st 9 days. *Nau Durga.*

The first nine nights of *Chait* are dedicated to the goddess Parvati, the wife of Siva. On the eighth day food cooked in *ghee* is eaten in the household and is shared by the menials who receive pay in kind. Five or seven virgins (not outcastes) are fed. They are given ground parched gram first and then food cooked in *ghee.* The florists in charge of the *Devi*† temple 3½ miles from Karimpur are the ones who profit most from these days. Each family from the surrounding villages offers from 2 to 4 ounces of grain, 8 small *puris* and a pice or two.

April 12—10th day. *Khan Bahadur ka Mela.*

On a hillock at the edge of Karimpur there is the tomb of Khan Bahadur, "a famous chief who lived about a century and a half ago" (*Mainpuri Gazeteer*, page 217, edition 1910). On this date a small religious fair is held. Women of various castes go to the tomb and make offerings of grain, pice and sweets on a cloth which the Faqirs of the village spread over the tomb. The Faqirs beat drums to attract people to the *Mela*‡, and collect the offerings made to the tomb. The grain parcher of the village sells *laddus*§ of rice and raw sugar, *batasas*, gram, puffed rice and tobacco. The bangle-seller sells bracelets, the vege-

*NOTE: There is no agreement between the lunar month and the Gregorian calendar, hence actual dates are given for one year to show the approximate time of the year.

†Devi—goddess.

‡Mela—religious fair.

§Laddu—a sweetmeat made in the form of a ball.

table grower sells cucumbers, and the village shop-keeper sells various kinds of sweets. The local men strive to make the *Mela* a big occasion but it attracts very little attention outside of Karimpur.

April 18 to May 1, 1927. *Baisakh* (Dark Half) (From day after full moon through new moon).

April 20. 3rd day, *Kuberpur Mela.*

The village people go to a temple located at Kuberpur, one mile from the village. The florist of Karimpur receives the offerings made to the figure of *Mahadev*, which is kept in this temple.

May 2 to May 16, 1927. *Baisakh* (Light Half).

May 4. 3rd day. *Akhtij* Celebration of the beginning of the present world age. A small clay tumbler of ground parched gram is given to each "kam karnewala" for religious merit.

May 17—May 30, 1927. *Jeth* (Dark Half) (14 days in this half). Nothing special.

May 31—June 15, 1927. *Jeth* (Light Half) (16 days in this half).

June 9th. 10th day. *Ganges Dasehra.* The last of the ten days generally observed at the time when "the stream of the Ganges first fell on the head of the god Siva." (*Rites of the Twice-Born*, Stevenson, page 298.)

In the village on this day, the faithful eat food cooked in *ghee*, which is shared by the menials who receive pay in kind.

June 10th. 11th day. *Bhim Ekadasi.*

This is a special fast day observed by most castes. Occasionally on this date a complete outfit of clothes is given to the pundit. Sometimes it is a man's outfit consisting of a shirt, *dhoti**, hat and shoes or a woman's outfit consisting of a skirt, vest, scarf, bracelets, anklets, the brass mark to be placed on the forehead and gum for sticking it on, the red colour for the part in the hair, and wax for fixing the colour.

June 16—June 29, 1927. *Asarh.* (Dark Half) (14 days in this half). Nothing special. On the 15th day—new moon—no ploughing is done.

June 30 to July 14, 1927. *Asarh* (Light Half)

July 14. *Puranmashi. Asarh ki Mela* at the Devi grounds, Mainpuri.

On this day the village people go to the Devi grounds and make their offerings of a few pice, some small *puris* and 2 to 4 ounces of grain. This is an auspicious day for having boys receive their first hair cut. The village barber may do it, or barbers who are present at the *Mela.* (See First Hair cutting, page 56 as above.) Food cooked in *ghee* is eaten in the houses of the faithful and the "kam karnewalas" share.

July 15—July 28, 1927. *Sawan* (Dark Half) (14 days in this half.) Nothing special.

July 29—August 13, 1927. *Sawan* (Light Half) (16 days in this half).

July 31. 3rd day. *Teejan.*

On this day *Simai*† and *Khir*‡ are made specially. These together with *puris* are shared with the "kam karnewalas". The florist supplies henna and receives 11 ounces of grain.

August 2. 5th day. *Nag panchami.*

---

*Dhoti—loin cloth 3 to 5 yards in length.

†Simai—spaghetti.

‡Khir—rice cooked in milk.

Barley and wheat seeds are sown in several earthenware jars. The earth is taken from a prospective barley field.

August 13. *Puranmashi. Sanuna* or *Raksha bandhan.* On this date, the bard places the coloured cotton bracelet on the wrists of his jajmans, for which he receives 11 ounces of grain and from 2 to 4 pice. The florist supplies henna for staining the feet of the ladies of the jajman's family and receives 11 ounces of grain. All of the employees receive a handful of *Simai*, cooked with raw sugar, one or two *puris* and 1 or 2 *Dal ki kachoris**. During this half of the month in case a wedding has occurred during the previous year, 3 or 4 Rupees worth of sweets together with a complete outfit of clothes is taken by the water-bearer or the water-bearer and barber to the bride's home. Upon delivery they each receive a Rupee, and one Rupee is given by the recipient for the sender.

August 14—August 27, 1927. *Bhadon* (Dark Half). (14 days in this half).

August 20. 8th day. *Janamashtami.* Commemorating the birth of Kirshna.

The pundit of the village receives 8 to 12 annas which are offered at the time of the community celebration.

August 28 to September 11, 1927. *Bhadon* (Light half).

August 29. 2nd day. *Kurane ki puja*, (special worship for Siva).

September 2. 6th day. *Dev Chhat* held at Parson, Etah District.

This *Mela* is of special significance only to the

---

*Dal ki kachoris—lentil filled turnovers.

carpenters who take yokes, wooden plates, door frames and carts to Parson for sale.

September 10. 14th day. *Anant Chaudas.* Day of putting on *Ant* (an armlet made of 14 threads and containing 14 knots.)

Food cooked in *ghee* is eaten in the household on this day and is shared with the household "kam karnewalas".

September 12 to September 25, 1927. *Kuar* (Dark Half) (14 days in this half).

Entire half. *Kanagat.* The obsequial ceremonies which take place in the sign of Virgo.

Each family worships its ancestors on the day of the half month on which they died. On each day a death has occurred, as many Brahmans are fed as deaths occurred. In the village only two generations of deaths are remembered. In the case of the poor, Brahmans are fed only on the 15th day, which is *Amawas.* On the days on which Brahmans are fed, only food cooked in *ghee* is eaten in the household and this shared with the household "kam karnewalas".

September 26 to October 10, 1927. *Kuar* (Light Half).

September 26—October 5. 1st 9 days. *Nau Durga* (*Dasehra*) (Only the 8th day specially observed in Karimpur).

On the 8th day food cooked in *ghee* is eaten in the household and shared with household employees. in addition 5 to 7 virgins of any caste other than outcastes are fed. They are first given ground parched gram and then food cooked in *ghee.*

October 10. *Puranmashi. Khir* and occasionally sweets are placed in the open over night so that *Amirth* (immortal properties) may fall on it. This gives the food special strengthening properties.

October 11 to October 25, 1927. *Katik* (Dark Half).

October 13. 3rd day. *Karua Chauth.*

On this day the florist's wife is given a *puri*, and the washerman's wife is given *Bhat** and *Jor* (buttermilk and gram flour). All others receive 2 thin or one thick *chapati*. The washerman's wife receives the grain which is offered in worship to the drawing on the wall.

October 25. *Amawas. Bari Divali.*

On *Divali* the florist receives 11 ounces of grain in return for flowers presented. All the "kam karnewalas" receive food cooked in *ghee*, one or two large *puris* and 1 or 2 *Dal Kachoris*, together with a double handful of puffed rice, 7 or 8 *batasas* and a small figure made out of sugar, called a *ghora*.

(NOTE:—On holidays like this, not only the "kam karnewalas" who do daily work for the jajman, are entitled to a hand-out but all of the "kam karnewalas" in the village who can lay the slightest claim on the jajman.

October 26—November 9, 1927. *Katik* (Light Half).

October 26. 1st day. *Gobardhan.*

Sometimes there is food cooked in *ghee* in the household which is shared with household "kam karnewalas."

October 27. 2nd day. *Bhaiya Deoj.*

From the time of marriage, on this day, sweets are sent by the head of the house to the homes of each married woman in the household. These sweets are sent as gifts to the women's brothers. The barber and the water-bearer are the messengers. Upon delivery of sweets valued at 1 or 2 Rupees, the recipient doubles the value in cash and

*Bhat—cooked rice.

sends it to the sender. He also gives the bearers of the sweets food for their return journey and 8 annas or 1 Rupee in cash.

November 5. 11th day. *Deothan.* Beginning of the sugarcane harvest.

A farmer who has sugarcane planted sends five sugarcane stalks to each of his friends who have planted none. The messengers are a water-bearer's wife and a leather worker's wife. These women receive two pice from each recipient. All other caste people, chiefly "kam karnewalas" can get 10 to 12 canes if they are present in the field at the time the cane is cut.

November 9. *Puranmashi,* known as *Khatki puranmashi.*

Food cooked in *ghee* is eaten in the house and is shared with the household "kam karnewalas".

November 10 to November 24, 1927. *Aghan* (Dark Half). Nothing special.

November 25 to December 8, 1927. *Aghan* (Light Half). (14 days in this half.) Nothing special.

December 9 to December 24, 1927: *Pous* (Dark Half). (16 days in this half.)

Pous chahank is held at an auspicious time during the first half of the month as fixed by the head of the household. On this day food cooked in *ghee* is eaten and is shared with household "kam karnewalas".

Makara Sakrant is likewise held when appointed by the pundits. It may fall in the light half as well. On this day 1¾ pounds of rice is sent to the priest.

December 25 to January 7, 1928. *Pous* (Light Half). (14 days in this half.) Nothing special unless *Makara Sakrant* falls in this half.

January 8 to January 23, 1928. *Magh* (Dark Half) (16 days in this half).

January 10. 3rd day. *Sakat.*

On this day 1 or 2 large *puris*, 1 or 2 *dal kachoris*, 1 *pitowa* (bajra flour, raw sugar, and sesamum seed cooked in oil or *ghee*), and 1 *laddu* made of millet, sorghum or rice are given to each of the "kam karnewalas".

January 24 to February 6, 1928. *Magh* (Light Half). (14 days in this half).

January 28. 5th day. *Basant.*

The bard presents each one of his jajmans with green barley sticks. In exchange, he is given 11 ounces of grain and a few pice. Some families have food cooked in *ghee* on this day, which is shared with the household "kam karnewalas".

February 7 to February 21, 1928. *Phagon* (Dark Half).

February 19. 13th day. *Shiv Teras.* Fast day for women.

About noon on this day the wife of the florist comes to a village image of *Mahadev* with flowers. She stays there for several hours and receives the offerings of the women to *Mahadev.* The women offer *Ber* (zizyphus jujuba) fruit, a pice, two or three ounces of grain and some small pieces of sugar cane.

February 22 to March 6, 1928. *Phagon* (Light Half) (14 days in this half).

March 6. *Puranmashi. Holi.*

The barber shows all of his customers a looking glass and receives from 5 to 11 ounces of grain or 1 or 2 pice. The florist supplies flowers and gets a similar gift. The barber, carpenter, washerman, water-bearer and potter each receive 24 ounces of raw sugar on this day. The leather worker receives half that amount. If the sweeper, seamster, mat-maker and cotton carder come for raw sugar they get about as much as is given to the leather worker. In addition they receive 1 or 2 large *puris*, 1 or 2 *Dal kachoris*, 1 or 2 *Goja**, 2 *assi*†, 1 *battu* (a kind of *laddu* made from gram), and 4 *khajuria* (made of wheat and gur, triangular in shape). Food cooked in *ghee* is eaten in the house and is shared with the "kam karnewalas" of the household. The shepherd, faqir, grain parcher, florist and dancing girl are given *puris* and *Dal Kachora.*

March 7 to March 22, 1928. *Chait* (Dark Half) (16 days in this half).

March 7. 1st day. *Rangdhul.* Food cooked in *ghee* is eaten by some families and is shared with their household "kam karnewalas".

March 8. 2nd day. *Kurane ki puja.*

March 14. 8th day. *Devi ka mela.*

Offerings are made at the *Devi* temple, Mainpuri, as has already been noted, and food cooked in *ghee* is eaten in some households. On most special days the bangle seller finds ready sale for his glass bracelets. The women never lose an opportunity to acquire a few more.

March 23—April 5, 1928. *Chait* (Light Half) (See page 61).

Occasionally there occurs an eclipse of the sun or moon. This is a time of special value to the sweepers. One of the traditions current in Karimpur is that at the

*Goja— a semi-circular sweet meat made of wheat flour, filled with spices and sugar.

†Assi—ground rice and raw sugar mixed and cooked in oil.

beginning of the world, God wanted to provide his people with seed so that they could plant various kinds of grain. As God had no seed, he borrowed it from Graha, a cesspool cleaner. After some time Graha requested God to pay him back what he owed, but he could not. Thereupon Graha seized him by the arms. As his touch meant defilement, God slashed off the flesh that had been touched. These pieces of flesh fell on the sun or moon and caused an eclipse. From time to time when Graha seizes God, this experience is repeated. In order to help God to meet his obligations incurred on their behalf, and to free him from this suffering, the villagers give their cesspool cleaners about $\frac{1}{3}$ pound of grain on the morning after the eclipse. The actual income of 5 cesspool cleaner families at the time of eclipse of the moon on December 8, 1927 is herewith given.

Family A received 11 pounds of grain from one Karimpur jajman and a few jajmans in a nearby village.

Family B received 74 pounds of grain. 6 Brahman jajmans, 2 Kyasth, 1 Bhat, 5 Kachhis, 1 Kahar, 1 Barhai and 1 Teli each gave $\frac{1}{3}$ pound of grain; 2 Gadariyas, 1 Dhuna, 1 Kahar, 2 Barhais, 1 Darzi and 1 Brahman each gave $\frac{1}{6}$ pound. One Brahman gave $\frac{1}{2}$ pound. The remaining quantity was received from four other nearby villages.

Family C received $31\frac{1}{2}$ pounds of grain from the following: 4 Brahmans, 1 Sunar, 1 Kachhi, 2 Kahars and 1 Barhai each gave $\frac{1}{3}$ pound. One Brahman gave $\frac{1}{6}$ pound. The balance came from 4 nearby villages.

Family D received 42 pounds. 4 Brahmans, 2 Kachhis, 1 Kahar and 2 Manihars each gave $\frac{1}{3}$ pound. 1 Brahman and 5 Kachhis each gave $\frac{1}{6}$ pound. The balance came from 4 nearby villages.

Family E received 13 pounds. 5 Brahmans, 1 Kahar, 1 Bharbhunja, and 1 Kumhar each gave $\frac{1}{3}$ pound. 1 Kahar and 1 Darzi each gave $\frac{1}{6}$ pound. The balance came from 1 nearby village.

The Mohammedan holidays and ceremonies observed in the village yield very little to the employee population. When a *Charpai* is needed for a wedding, the village carpenter gets the trade; when clay jars and clay cups are needed, the village potter furnishes them; when special washing has to be done, the washerman does it; and the barber attends to their shaving. The sweepers are the only ones in the village who will touch their food and they take the left-overs when there is any special feast.

C. Concessions

The rights of the "kam karnewala" do not cease when the carpenter has received his bi-yearly 14 pounds of grain, the water-bearer his bi-yearly 8.4 pounds of grain, the washerman his 21 pounds of grain and occasional *chapati*, or the cesspool cleaner his daily *chapati*. Were this the extent of their rights they would be attracted elsewhere by offers of higher pay. The concessions made available to them in living in Karimpur offset for them any advantages that would appear to be theirs if they were to be employed in a city environment at reasonable fixed wages. A large part of the strength of the Hindu Jajmani system is inherent in this practice of making concessions to "kam karnewalas". According to the Laws of Manu, the Brahmans must provide suitable maintenance for the Sudras*. "The remnants of their food must be given to him, as well as their old clothes, the refuse of their grain, and their old household furniture." (X:125).

*See page 72.

1. Free Residence site

The "kam karnewalas" in the village have been given free residence sites on which they have built their mud-walled houses. These houses are grouped together around the area occupied by the one time owners of the village, namely the Brahmans. The "kam karnewala" has clearly defined rights and limitations to the residence site given to him. The *Wajib-ul-arz** of Karimpur, Chapter IV, Rule 2, states, "They can build or repair their old house on the land in their possession, but they cannot build a new house on a new land without the permission of the Landlord". (Translated by Mr. Salig Ram, *Sadar Kanungo*, Headquarters Record Clerk of Mainpuri.) And again, Chapter IV, Rule 3, states, "The tenants in these villages (reference includes the other habitats within the Karimpur revenue village area) have no right to sell or mortgage or hypothecate the house of their residence, nor does the landlord have a right to sell the house of a cultivator or non-cultivator in which he lives. If a cultivator or non-cultivator is absconded from the village, his house will be the property of the Landlord. If a tenant flies away from the village on acount of some natural calamity and comes back within a year, his residential house will be returned to him. The house of one who dies without an heir or an absconded tenant will pass into the hands of the Landlord." Not only do the "kam karnewalas" of Karimpur have free land for their residence, but, with the exception of only one leather worker family, they also have well water for their use within fifty yards of their own houses. These wells were dug with the help of prosperous jajmans.

*Wajib-ul-arz—customary law of a village, a copy of which is kept in the District Headquarters.

2. Free timber

(a) For house building and house repairs

The only material of value put into a Karimpur house, is the timber used for the beams, door frames, and doors. If the house is to be built of mud, and the majority of them are, the earth is dug from a nearby pit or one newly dug for the purpose. If sun baked bricks are to be used, they are formed and dried in a nearby clay field. The necessary timber is available in various ways. The *Wajib-ul-arz*, Chapter IV, Rule 3, states, "And from the trees on the *Usar* *and unculturable land, they can take wood for the use of their implements and repair of houses upon permission from the Landlord."

The "kam karnewala" usually gets the wood used in repair work by approaching his jajman in the attitude of a supplicant, as an inferior approaching a superior. He makes his request in a most submissive manner by bowing before the jajman with folded hands, touching his forehead. This posture is called *hath jhorke* which means literally folded hands. It is more dignified than begging, but involves a recognition of subserviency. It is a form of Hindu greeting most generally used whether it be as between equals or between unequals. One can get the true significance of it only when one understands the relationship existing between the one who is greeted and the one who does the greeting. In the relationship between "kam karnewala" and jajman, it is *not* as between equals.

Occasionally the "kam karnewalas" have a few trees of their own which they are free to use. "Tenants

*Usar—land infested with various salts.

are the owners of the trees in their fields and houses (planted by them) and have the right to sell them." (*Wajib-ul-arz*, Chapter IV, Rule 4.) Of the "kam karnewalas" in the social scale lower than the vegetable grower and rice grower, only one water bearer family and the two bangle seller families have trees of their own sufficient to meet their own needs. One carpenter family, the barber family, two water bearer families, one tradesman family, one leather worker family and one cotton-carder family have a few trees but not enough to meet their needs. It is necessary, therefore, for the large majority of the "kam karnewalas" to go to their jajmans for timber.

(*b*) *For implements*

Chapter IV, Rule 3 of the *Wajib-ul-arz* as quoted above includes "wood for the use of their implements". The beam of the plough takes the largest piece of wood recognized under this rule. Most of the wood needed for implements goes into handles, for which very little is required.

(*c*) *For fuel*

Dead branches may be broken off, and branches or twigs scattered about on the ground can be picked up and taken home. A favourite method of gathering wood is to fasten a small knife to the end of a long bamboo pole, and then hack off dead branches. They are not always dead, however. The shepherd constantly hacks off green branches so that his goats can have leaf food. The goats clean up the leaves while the branches are left to dry and be picked up by some one looking for fuel. Although the village housewife prefers wood for fuel, there is not enough available for all. Therefore she uses cow-dung largely, of which more will be said later.

(*d*) *For cremation*

All Hindus are cremated—with the exception of babies, who are buried. The cremation takes place within a few hours after death. The fuel for cremation may be largely dung cakes. In addition, there must be two large chunks of wood to weigh down the hips of the corpse, and enough wood to insure a good bed of coals. This fuel for cremation is always available for a "kam karnewala". One or more jajmans are ready to meet this urgent requirement without cost to him. Were the "kam karnewala" resident in a town or city, he would find this item of fuel for cremation a considerable expense.

3. Free food

(*a*) *Greens*

The "kam karnewala" may have various kinds of *sag** if he cares to pluck them. One variety or another is available in all but two months of the year. They may be listed as those that grow wild, as flowers or buds from trees which are used as greens, and as those available from cultivated fields.

Those that grow wild may be listed as follows:

August, September and October	1. Muniya (?)†
	2. Paintiya (?)
	3. Lissua (Triumfetta pilosa)
	4. Nari (?)
	5. Mushrooms
	6. Chonraiya (Amaranthus viridis)
October	Wild Rice
November, December and January	Bathua (Chenopodium album)
April and May	Simara-gutha (?)

*Sag—leafy vegetables and green herbs used as pottage.

†(?) Scientific name not known.

Flowers or buds from trees which are used as greens may be listed as follows:

April and May	Mauwa (Bassia Latifolia)
June and July	1. Tamarind (Tamarindus Indica)
	2. Kachnar (Bauhinia Variegata)
	3. Khata Labhera (Cordia myxa)
	4. Rai Labhera (Cordia vestita)
	5. Gular (Ficus glomerata)

Those which are available from cultivated fields may be listed as follows:

October	1. Darhari (Cyamopsis psoralioides)
	2. Ronsa (Vegna Catjang)
December, January and February	Green coriander
January and February	1. Sarson tops (Brassica juncea)
	2. Channa tops (Cicer arietinum)
	3. Mattar tops (Dolichos biflorus)

The greens that grow wild and the buds or flowers from trees are gathered by the "kam karnewalas" when in season and available. The tops of growing plants and in some cases pods and grain may be broken off from time to time by "kam karnewalas", so long as the quantity taken is not larger than is required for a small mess for a family. This is not theft. It is the right of a "kam karnewala".

(*b*) *Fruit*

The "kam karnewalas" also have the privilege of gathering fruit. Access to fruit trees is forbidden in only a few cases in Karimpur. Hence whatever fruit is available is shared by all who happen to be interested in collecting some for themselves. The variety of fruit trees in the village is large but the number of all trees is not great enough so that everyone can have every fruit. Some fruits like mangoes and *bers* which are most numerous are found in the homes of all. One grove of twenty-five old trees, bearing in a good season upward of 50,000 mangoes, is open to all comers. Many of the other fruits are brought home, either by a member of the family who has chanced upon a tree of a particular fruit, or who has gone out in search of whatever could be found. Many of the fruits are eaten as they are picked up at the tree and never reach the house of the finder. The fact remains, however, that there are a large number of trees of which the fruit is eaten and to such an extent that many an aching void is satisfied. The trees listed below furnish edible fruit. This list does not include the specially cultivated fruits like grafted mangoes, guavas, custard apples and the like.

These fruits are all available in the months of April, May, June or July.

1. Mango (Mangifera India)
2. Bargat (Ficus Bengalensis)
3. Pipal (Ficus Religiosa)
4. Neem (Melia Azadirachta)
5. Jaman (Eugenia Jambolana)
6. Khata Labhera (Cordia Myxa)
7. Rai Labhera (Cordia Vestita)
8. Khajur (Phaenix Dactylifera)
9. Heens (Capparis Sepiera)
10. Kundru (Boswellia Glabra)
11. Kait (Feronia Elephantum)
12. Ber (Zizyphus jujuba)
13. Imli (Tamarindus Indica)
14. Mauwa (Bassia Latifolia)
15. Bel (Aegle Marmelos)
16. Gular (Ficus Glomerata)

(*c*) *Grain*

(*1*) *Wild Rice*

The poorer of the "kam karnewalas" when not otherwise occupied spend a share of their time during September and October in the low marshland near the village harvesting wild rice. No figures for the actual amount harvested are available but we found that the sweepers for instance, were using this wild rice almost exclusively during September and October. In their usual

Sunday grain offerings to the local church they contributed mostly wild rice.

(2) *Gleanings*

The leather workers have the privilege of gleaning the wheat and barley fields in which they have assisted in making the irrigation beds. This is true especially of the fields owned by Brahman jajmans. The sweeper women and children then follow after the first gleaning and have little trouble in collecting a pound or two of grain each. On March 27, 1928, one adult woman (a wife of a shepherd) picked up 2⅝ pounds of *bali** of wheat and barley in about five hours time. She had a good sized basket crowded full. A small boy who had been out but a short time had 13½ ounces of *bali*. We ourselves broke up the *bali* and found 3½ ounces *bhusa*† and 10 ounces grain. At this rate, the adult woman got 31 1/9 ounces out of 2⅝ pounds or roughly two pounds of grain for five hours work. When it is taken home it has to be broken up and cleaned. It is of interest to note that the harvester earns 7 to 8 2/5 pounds for work all day. At this rate, the gleaner can pick up about one-third of what the day labourers can earn by harvesting. The gleaners must follow close on the heels of the harvesters or be in the fields before the birds and animals come the morning after. Otherwise they find no gleanings. Other "kam karnewalas" in addition to the leather workers and sweepers join in the gleaning if they need to supplement their store of grain.

(3) *Outright Gift of Grain*

"Kam karnewalas" who have no special rights, if in need of food, can come *hath jhorke* and be certain of

*Bali—the ear of cereals

†Bhusa—chaff

receiving some grain. Such people go to the fields for crops harvested in the spring and to the threshing floors for crops harvested in the autumn. In the subconscious mind of the good Hindu there is always the thought "a giver of grain (receives) Eternal bliss." (Manu IV: 232.)

(*d*) *Cooked food and raw sugar*

In the same manner a "kam karnewala" is certain of getting cooked food or raw sugar when it is available in any quantity. When a well was being made, thirty villagers were lending a hand. The owner of the well supplied them with as much raw sugar as they could eat. A sweeper, who because of his untouchability, was not allowed to share in the work, presented himself for his share and got it. Washerman youngsters were also on hand and received enough to make them happy.

4. Free Clothing

Second hand clothes of all kinds are frequently available if the "kam karnewala" chooses to ask for them. It may be a barber or it may be a sweeper. Each feels free to ask his jajman when necessity arises. The fear that some have, lest someone see them wearing second hand clothes, is not shown by the "kam karnewalas". Instead, there is a smug satisfaction in that the clothes which were formerly worn by one of the Twice-Born, may bring to them special protection.

(*a*) *Grazing rights*

5. Free Food For Animals

The villager is not happy without livestock. All but 29 families had some stock in 1927. These families without stock included three Brahman, one goldsmith, two vegetable growers, six water-bearers, one shepherd, two seamsters, one oil-presser, three mat-makers, two leather-workers, four sweepers, three Faqir families, and one dancing girl. Among them were people who were too old to take care of stock, some who were temporarily wihout them and others too poor to have them. But some of all castes had animals. They spend the minimum on feed for their animals as they trust largely to grazing for other than work animals. This grazing they get free. The *Wajib-ul-arz*, Chapter II, Rule 15, states, "The village cattle graze on the *usar* land without any charge. And this will continue hereafter also." The *usar* is not the only grazing land in the villages. Fields that lie fallow, newly cut fields, uncultivated land, and land that is often covered with water are available for use. Grazers of sheep and goats are permitted to break off green leaves from the trees. Although the milk supply given by these animals is very small, the villager who goes to the city feels very much its restrictions which do not permit him to keep animals.

(*b*) *Fodder*

After a harvest each "kam karnewala" has accumulated a small quantity of fodder for the animals. Some of it has been obtained as wages for field labour, some as part of the bi-yearly wages in kind, and, in the case of some as for example the sweeper, it has been obtained *hath jhorke*. The Laws of Manu III: 95, state, "A twice-born householder gains by giving alms, the same reward for his meritorious act which (a student) obtains for presenting, in accordance with the rule, a cow to his teacher." Within a month's time one Brahman family gave a day's fodder to a goldsmith, an oil-presser, a carpenter and a barber, simply because they had asked for it. Grass is available in various places for the cutting. It may not be the choicest, but it helps to keep animals from starving. A regular late afternoon occupation is for the villagers to go out to the uncultivated fields with their spuds and scrape off the grass which is often too short for an animal to graze. This continues until all vegetation is gone—at the beginning of the hot season. When there is a shortage of green grass and weeds the farmers strip leaves for their cattle just as the shepherds do for their goats. When a wedding party comes to the house of one of the "kam karnewalas" and there are oxen with the party, the host finds no difficulty in *hath jhorke* acquiring the fodder necessary to feed the visiting animals. The needs of the "kam karnewala" are met and he is happy. He little realizes how much he is dependent on these small favours until he has antagonized the jajmans and they suddenly refuse to supply those things which the "kam karnewala" has come to consider as his rights.

6. Free Dung

(*a*) *For fuel*

The expenditure the villager begrudges most in the city is that for fuel. Ordinarily he has to buy no less than 1½ maunds (123 pounds) of wood per month per person at a cost of not less than 1 Rupee. Cow-dung fuel cakes are seldom available. If he is in a city like Kanpur where on a Sunday he can track out into the country and collect wood and cow-dung for the week's fuel, he is not so unhappy. But what can compare with the convenience of the village supply? There is cow and buffalo-dung everywhere, which the members of the family can always accumulate and make into the much favoured fuel cakes. And it costs them nothing. The families with their own cattle have a constant supply on hand and the poor without cattle can go out and gather it from the grazing grounds and road sides.

(*b*) *For plastering walls and floors*

The woman plasters her cooking place freshly every day with mud and cow-dung. The place of worship in the courtyard is plastered for each special occasion. And two times in the year *Diwali* and *Holi*, when there is a general house cleaning, all floors, and the walls inside and outside the house are freshly plastered. None in the village lack for the necessary materials. They are free for the collecting.

(*c*) *For manure*

The farmers use some of the dung of the village for manure for some of their fields. The amount used is governed by the scanty supply on hand. It is used chiefly by those who have animals of their own. But here again if a "kam karnewala" has no manure or insufficient manure of his own, he is free to collect what he can find wherever he can find it. Apart from fuel cakes which are made and sometimes sold to the potters, no dung is sold in the village. It is the common property of all.

7. Rent Free Land

Khidmati-muafi, or rent free land, is another perquisite of the village "kam karnewala". Land owners in the past have made it possible for village "kam karnewalas" to supplement their earnings by giving them a small piece of land to cultivate. For this no rent is charged and the employee is expected to render a particular type of service in the village. The Tenancy Act III of 1926, Section

183 states, "A rent-free grant means a grant of a right to hold land rent-free by a landlord with or without consideration." The *Wajib-ul-arz*, Chapter II, Rule 12, states, "The land which is given rent-free will remain so as long as the servce is done by the holder." That is to say, so long as the carpenter continues to do carpentry work in the village he will continue to be the cultivator of that particular bit of rent-free land. The castes that have rent-free land in the village with the amount each has are herewith listed.

Florist 2.2.—Acres Grove land	.19	acres	cultivable	land
Oil-Presser	.86	acres	,,	,,
Washerman	.41	acres	,,	,,
Carpenter	1.34	acres	,,	,,
Seamster	.87	acres	,,	,,
Sweeper	1.15	acres	,,	,,
Brahman for lighting *Holi* fire	2.33	acres	,,	,,

(A slight rent is now being taken from the Brahman.) One of the Faqir families holds 1.81 acres, which was given to them as an outright gift. No one can take it away from them.

8. Credit Facilities

The worthy "kam karnewala" is always assured of loans at the current rate of interest, which ranges from 12 per cent to 16 per cent on large loans and 24 per cent on small loans. These loans are available (1) for the purchase of land rights, (2) for agricultural purposes—purchase of seed, hire of labour and occasionally for equipment, such as a sugarcane press, (3) for livestock, and (4) for religious ceremonies and festivals. The seamster can borrow enough to enable him to purchase a sewing machine and the sweeper enough to buy some pigs. The rate of interest always bears a direct ratio to the risk involved by the transaction. When a sweeper buys pigs, the jajman can easily see whether the pigs were bought and he knows when they are sold. He incurs very little risk in such a transaction, and he can lend the money at the current rate of 24 per cent. When rates higher than this are charged it is generally because the loan is taken for other than productive purposes, or the one who borrows is not a good risk. A gambler for instance might be expected to pay two annas per month per Rupee or at the rate of 130 per cent. In the city undue advantage may be taken of a man's adversity. But in the village the jajman knows that it is his "kam karnewala" or his "kam karnewalas'" sons who will serve him and his sons, and there is nothing to be gained in alienating them through making life in the village unbearable, or in permitting them to obligate themselves to people outside the village. The average village "kam karnewala's" money needs are very few and when they are pressing, he can always find a jajman in Karimpur who is prepared to help him.

9. Opportunities for supplementary employment

(a) *For men*

The "kam karnewala" living in the village, not only has a chance of working at his trade but he also gets opportunities for agricultural work. At the time of sowing, weeding, irrigating and harvesting when labour is scarce and his own work is not pressing, he can find opportunities for supplementing his food store. Or he may share in fields. One method is for a "kam karnewala" who owns neither oxen nor plough to take 4/5 of an acre of land from a Brahman jajman for the purpose of planting sorghum. The Brahman jajman furnishes the oxen and seed and pays the rent. The co-sharer furnishes the labour. The owner of the field gets ¾ of the crop and the co-sharer ¼. Another method arises when a jajman sees that he cannot handle the weeding of a certain maize field. He contracts with a "kam karnewala" to handle the weeding and harvesting, for which he is entitled to ¼ of the crop. Where the "kam karnewala" has oxen he can enter into equal shares with others in crops, because he can supply both oxen and labour. Other opportunities come to the "kam karnewala" such as rope-making, roof-making and repairing, wall-making and repairing, and occasionally the making of sun-dried bricks and the digging of a well. Every hot season, philanthropically minded Brahmans employ several water-bearers to draw water at advantageous points along the roadside so that thirsty travellers and thirsty animals may find water to drink.

(*b*) *For Women*

When a "kam karnewala" is in need of assistance he can generally find some one who wants grain ground. The women folk of the family can render aid in this way. They are paid at the rate of one anna or 1 2/5 pounds of grain for every seven pounds ground, representing an hour and a half's work. For grinding maize, which is more difficult, they are paid at the rate of 1½ annas or 2 1/10 pounds of grain for grinding seven pounds. The walls of jajman's houses must be plastered from time to time with dung. Three and one half pounds of grain plus one good meal is given for doing this work. The bulk of this kind of work is done by leather workers and mat-maker women except when a jajman wants one who is indebted to him financially, to give some assistance. Leather worker and vegetable grower women assist as day labourers in cutting the rains crops and help in the sowing of the winter crops. They are paid 7 pounds of grain for harvesting and 7 pounds of grain plus one meal for sowing. During cotton picking season some of the women get a chance to pick cotton. They have to pick over the field every three days during the ripening season. A woman is given one-tenth of what she picks as her wage.

10. Free use of tools, implements and draft animals

The "kam karnewala" needs to own no tools or agricultural implements unless he intends to make a business of agriculture. When he cultivates an acre or less he can generally get along by borrowing the necessary tools and implements from his jajmans. The sweeper, the barber, and the washerman in Karimpur may be seen threshing their grain. Where did they get their oxen? They borrowed them. Ordinary implement needs, such as ploughs, irrigation buckets, well tackle, spade, sickle, etc. are met in this way. Hence the lack of such things in the homes of many village employees. If a sweeper is so ill that he needs to go to the hospital, no one will give him space in his ox cart. But if an ox cart can be spared, a sweeper may have the loan of oxen and cart so that he may take his relative to the desired destination.

11. Free use of raw materials

The "kam karnewalas" may have their earnings in the village supplemented by making baskets for sale, as do the leather workers and sweepers, by making mats and fans as do the mat-makers, or by making dung fuel cakes. The baskets are made from *arhar* (Cytians cajan) stalks, which are available only in the fields of certain farmers. When the farmers have no special need for the staiks in household repairs, they are usually willing to give them to the sweepers and leather workers. In the case of poorer farmers a small price is given. The mat-makers have no difficulty in getting a supply sufficient for local needs of *Khajur* (Phaenix Dactylifera) leaves for making fans and mats. Mention has already been made as to the availability of dung for making dung fuel cakes. The supply of these raw materials which cost only the labour of collection, enables the "kam karnewala" to realize on both the value of materials and his labour. In reality the prices received for the finished products are so low that he realizes very little more than the value of labour involved in collection, manufacture and distribution. The carpenters are permitted to strip the bark from trees which they cut down, and to keep the odd pieces of wood which accumulate in the course of their work. Certain kinds of bark such as the *Acacia Arabica* are sold for tanning purposes while others are used for fuel. The wood is made into charcoal and is used in their own forge fires or sold.

12. Free Hides

Dead animals, with the exception of pigs, are the property of the leather workers. The carcass, in case the animal dies at home, is taken to a field near the homes of the leather workers where it is skinned and the remainder left for vultures, hawks and village dogs. In former days the flesh of these animals was eaten by the leather workers. Now they will not eat the flesh of every animal. Some will eat none. Others use their discretion. The skin is washed with water and dried in the sun. No chemicals are applied, hence they cannot keep the skin for any length of time. They realize from the hide dealers five to six Rupees for a buffalo hide, and two to four Rupees for cow and bullock hides. Where a jajman is poor or of a grasping nature he may require the leather workers to give him a nominal fee for the carcass, one Rupee for a buffalo, eight annas for a bullock and four annas for a cow.

13. Free Funeral pyre plot

Each Hindu caste has its own place for cremation. The majority of these places are located on the *usar* land and no rent is paid for them. The Mohammedans, who bury their dead, have a common burial place of .07 acres which has the additional security of being recorded in the Government land records. Only one plot .04 acres is recorded for the Hindus although in actual practice each caste has its own customary place.

14. Casual leave

A great asset to some of the village "kam karnewalas" is that they can keep their jajmans and yet absent themselves for days, weeks or months. If an invitation comes from relatives for a feast, the "kam karnewala" may depute his work to his wife or a neighbour, and go cheerfully away. The washerman lost his wife. He told his low caste customers that until he got another wife he would be unabe to handle their washing. No one objected. Occasionally a sweeper or a mat-maker or a member of some other "kam karnewala" caste goes to Kanpur or Calcutta for work. He leaves a member of the family behind to attend to the minimum needs of his jajmans, earns a good income in the city and returns when he has had his fill. In every case the "kam karnewala" knows he will not lose his jajman. There are very few employees in cities who have so much freedom that they can leave their job, and yet keep it.

15. Aid in Litigation

There is generally some villager involved in a court case, which makes it necessary for him to go to Mainpuri, 5½ miles away, to attend one of the courts. Frequent postponements on one pretext or another cause one small case to be spread out over a long period. The "kam karnewala" when involved in a court case is as timid as a child, and gives his high caste jajmans no rest until one of them consents to go to court with him. There are always certain money transfers involved and consultations with petty lawyers who are looking after their own interests rather than those of the village client. The "kam karnewalas" look to their Brahman jajmans as being men of affairs, with whose help they hope ultimately to get justice. Hence some of the jajmans, who have become experienced in these court affairs, have to spend many days in a month helping "kam karnewalas". It is not altogether an unselfish service because it places the "kam karnewala" under various kinds of obligations to the helping jajman. Yet it is a service that the jajman is usually prepared to give and one that is very important to the illiterate and simple-minded "kam karnewala".

16. Variety in diet

One resident, a sweeper, in stating why he preferred to live in Karimpur on a low salary rather than in Calcutta on 25 to 30 Rupees per month, stated that in Calcutta he could get only a few of the staple foods to which he was accustomed, whereas in the village he could get a great variety of foods. He can have freshly parched heads of sorghum, millet, maize, wheat, barley, gram and peas. There is nothing more dear to the heart of the villager than to break off several heads of sorghum and parch them over the embers of a hastily made fire of twigs and broken bits of branches. There are several chutneys available that are prepared from local fruits. The *chapatis* vary season by season. They may be of maize, wheat, barley, millet, sorghum *bejar* (peas and barley) or *tihra* (wheat, gram, and barley). Five kinds of pulse are enjoyed in the village, namely, *mung*, *urad*, *moth*, *arhar* and *mattar*. There is raw sugar, sugarcane juice and the ever popular sugarcane. With a grain parcher in the village there is a plentiful supply of *chabena*, which is parched gram, maize, sorghum, millet, wheat, barley or pulse, and *satua* which is maize, sorghum or barley and peas together, parched, ground and mixed with water, milk or buttermilk. A villager working in a city thinks longingly of his village home as seasons come and go. Money cannot buy many of the foods dear to his village heart.

17. Healthful Location

An item of economic value which is only partly recognized by the "kam karnewalas" is the healthful location of their residence sites. The oil-pressers, seamsters, carpenters, mat-makers, shepherds, cotton carders, leather workers and sweepers all live on the edge of the village with the fresh air of the open country reaching them first. It was not the intention of Hindu society that the low caste people should have the choice residence sites, but that they be as far removed from them as possible, yet be close enough to afford them protection and perform their services. Now, as the value of fresh air and uncrowded spaces is more and more appreciated, it is evident that the low castes are really favoured in this respect. The leather workers of the village are most fortunate in that they have residence sites two hundred feet away from any other houses.

The health of no class of people suffers more than that of the Indian villager who goes to live in crowded tenements in a city. Hence the villager's reluctance to give up his village home.

II. Means of Maintenance.

The jajmani compensations and rights in Karimpur are maintained and supported by custom and the beliefs of the people themselves, the influcnce of the village elders, the Sacred Books of the Hindus and the Laws of the State.

A. Custom and Belief

The knowledge of the villagers regarding the functions and rights of the different occupational groups, as listed above, constitutes a body of customs which probably have more influence in maintaining the Hindu Jajmani System than any one other factor. Sir Henry Sumner Maine states:

> "What, in a primitive society, is the measure of Price? It can only be called custom. Although in the East influences destructive of the primitive notion are actively at work, yet in the more retired villages the artificer who plies an ancient trade still sells his wares for the customary prices, and would always change their quality rather than their price...It is of the very essence of custom, and this indeed chiefly explains its strength, that men do not clearly distinguish between their actions and their duties—what they ought to do is what they always have done, and they do it." (pages 190, 191 "Village Communities in the East and West.")

Custom is in part strengthened by the *Wajib-ul-arz* of Karimpur recorded in 1872, and to which several references have already been made. The customary law as recorded states the relationship which the Landlord bears to Karimpur and its residents. A further strengthening factor is the implicit belief of the people in this system.

The following Telegu story told by Mr. G. R. Subramiah Pantulu* serves as a good illustration of how a "kam karnewala" comes to look upon his position in Hindu society as being fixed and inalienable—a relationship which is so firmly established that no matter what happens to him his economic status is assured.

> "The king of Kalinga had a washerman who used to wash his clothes exceedingly well and bring and give them to him daily. One day, the king was exceedingly pleased with the scrupulously clean manner in which the clothes were brought to him and promised the washerman to grant any one prayer he might make. The washerman looked at the king and said that he was most anxious to become the king's minister and requested the king to bestow the post on him. The king did so, dispensing with the services of his old minister, who had served him for a very long time.
>
> "It came to pass that not long afterwards a certain other king, having heard of the weakness of the washerman minister, raised a huge army and gave battle. His master, having heard of what had come to pass, called upon the new minister to muster his forces, to which he replied that as he had already made the necessary preparations, there was no cause to fear the enemy. The king fully believed in this statement, but was sorely disappointed, for not long afterwards the city was attacked by the hostile armies. The king sent at once to the minister, told him what had happened and enquired of him as to the arrangements he had made.
>
> "The minister responded:—'There is nothing to fear in what has come to pass. But I find that the task of ruling a kingdom is a big affair, and while I was thinking of how best to rid ourselves of this difficulty, the enemy chanced to enter and blockade the city. Let them, therefore, undergo the perils of governing the kingdom. As for me, I used to wash the clothes of about a

*"184 Indian Tales," published by G. A. Natesan & Co., Madras, pages 195, 196.

> hundred families in this city; but since my elevation to the ministership, I have had to give up my calling. I will now, therefore, resume it and give you one-half the work and reserve the other half for myself; the calling being no trouble to me. On these considerations, I have made no preparations for war.'
>
> "The king was very much grieved when he heard this, but thought the result to be the natural punishment of linking himself to a fool."

The "kam karnewala's" knowledge of his customary function and rights is further strengthened by his beliefs which have been passed on to him through the generations. He may not be clear as to their source but they are an important motivating factor in his life. This may be illustrated by the following account:

Several years ago the government free school at Karimpur was closed because the villagers refused to allow their children to read in a school, in which we had entered a Christian boy known to the villagers by his old out-caste name, of *Bhangi*. The writer took an educated high-caste man to the school to interview the school teachers. We found one of the school teachers conversing with several *Ahirs*, cattlemen. They had come for transfer certificates for their boys. They wanted to have their boys transferred to a school some miles away. My friend asked them why they were so anxious to make their boys go to a school so much further away from their homes. They replied that they could not think of letting their boys read in a school along with *Bhangis*. He argued that there was no harm in letting the *Bhangis* read as well, and that the *Ahir* boys would not be required to touch the *Bhangis* or sit near to them. They answered that they could not consider it, because it was not intended by God that untouchables should read. Then they added, "And why if *Bhangis* are to read, have we all been created different? Why did God create carpenters, grain parchers, potters, barbers, cattlemen and the like? Did God not intend that each should perform his own work? And certainly it was not necessary for a *Bhangi* to read when his work was to clean cesspools." My friend, a town-bred Hindu, realized that the villagers' conception of caste and occupation was one that would be difficult to change.

B. The influence of the Village Elders

(1) IN RELATION TO THE "KAM KARNEWALA"

The first court of appeal in the village is the council of elders, or one or two of its members. Its greatest strength is in relation to the "kam karnewala". Cases decided by the council, which came to our attention while we were living in Karimpur, were as follows:

(*a*) It is the responsibility of one of the Brahman priests to light the *Holi* bonfire. All *Holi* festivities await the lighting of that fire. The priest was annoyed about something that had occurred to him and he refused to perform his duty. It will be remembered that he held a piece of property for the performance of this duty, although recently he has had to pay a nominal rent. All activities in the village were at a standstill while he sat. Various arguments were advanced as to why he should light the fire. In this way hours passed by. Two or three of the village elders talked it over among themselves. Finally the elder who had most influence over the priest said to him, "You had better go and light that fire now." And the priest went. The bonfire could have been started by other Brahmans in the village, but it was this man's duty and he was the one who had to do it.

(*b*) The shepherds have the right to graze their animals over the uncultivated lands of the villages. Occasionally an animal or two strays into a ripening field and causes some damage before the shepherd chases it out. On this occasion several animals were caught by an irate owner and brought to the house of one of the village elders. It was not long before the shepherd came to claim them. Various villagers who had grievances against the shepherd gathered at the elder's house and told the shepherd what they thought of him and all the rest of his caste. The shepherd could say nothing more than that he was sorry and would not let it occur again. The elder threatened that if this kind of charge did not cease, every shepherd would be put out of the village. After all had had their say and were tired of the word slaying, the animals were returned to the shepherd and he went to his house. The writer is doubtful whether after this event he was any more successful in keeping wandering animals from green pastures, but he had had an opportunity of hearing what his neighbours thought about him.

(*c*) In June 1927 the people of Karimpur were very much excited because the washerman had moved away. There was no one in the village who could wash their clothes. There were no other washermen in the village. Those who come into the village from the outside to do the work of a number of families could undertake no extra work. The Karimpur washerman had gone to the home of relatives where he intended to settle. His wife had died. He had no sons. One daughter was married and lived in another village with her husband. The other two daughters would soon have to be married and would leave him. He was very much depressed by his aloneness and the size of his jajmani, so he left the village. Messengers were sent by the village elders urging that he return at once, since the village was without the services of a washerman. He refused. As days ran into weeks more and more pressure was being put upon the village elders to act. They finally went in a body, five of them, to the neighbouring village to speak to the washerman in person. Some special offers of increased allowances were made to him and he consented to return. But his heart was not in it and he soon left again. Thereupon the elders, realizing that the fault was not on the side of the jajmans, arranged for a new washerman to come to Karimpur from a village where there were more washermen than necessary.

(2) In relation to the Jajman

The village Council of Elders, commonly known as the *Panchayat**, does not have the hold on the village people that it had prior to the introduction of an extensive court system. The autonomy of the village has in this way been impaired through the introduction of a centralized system of courts. As has been shown in the illustrations above, the *Panchayat* has a certain amount of influence over "kam karnewalas" but they no longer have the same influence over jajmans. Jajmans know that only Government courts can punish for violation of contract, so they pay little attention to what the *Panchayat* says. We saw several cases where the Council of Elders appeared to be helpless. They were unwilling to use the successful Indian method of boycotting the jajman. Within a caste, this would be legal. But under the present law a community-wide boycott could be construed as illegal restraint. The cases were as follows:

(*a*) One morning the writer was approached by a leather worker who had had his head cut open by a stone thrown by a Brahman jajman. The leather worker

*Panchayat—a body of arbitrators—usually five—assembled for the purpose of settling petty disputes among the people.

was about to start out to glean fields as was his right in return for making irrigation beds earlier in the season. The Brahman wanted him to help harvest his crop. The leather worker knew that if he did not glean he would lose his opportunity. Accordingly he refused. The jajman, in a fit of anger, threw a stone with such force that it cut the leather worker's head open. The *Panchayat* refused to take any action in this case. They heard the leather worker's story and said it was all "too bad," and that the jajman should be "spoken to," but that was the end of it.

(*b*) In the first Sawan (August) after a wedding, the members of a bridegroom's household send gifts to the bride who is at her own home. These gifts are carried by the barber and water-bearer. It is the custom for the conveyors of these gifts to receive three Rupees, one to be given to each of the messengers and one to the sending householder. On one occasion the barber and water-bearer on their return from delivering gifts to the bride's home, presented the 3 Rupees to their jajman so that he might keep a Rupee and give a Rupee to each one of them. He, however, kept 2 Rupees and gave them each 8 only annas, which was quite contrary to custom. The barber and water-bearer protested but the Brahman jajman kept the 2 Rupees. They had no redress.

(*c*) One of the grain parchers took a young buffalo from a Brahman jajman with the understanding that when the animal became full-grown he would get an equal share of the value of the buffalo. The grain parcher cared for the animal and when it was full-grown, the Brahman claimed it. No payment was made to the grain parcher and he had no way of enforcing the Brahman's promise, apart from law which is an expensive method for a poor man. Again this same Brahman got the grain parcher to share a field with him, the Brahman to furnish the oxen, seed and field, and the grain parcher the labour. The grain parcher carried out his share of the promise, but when the harvest time came he was not given a share. Here again he was unable to secure justice.

C. Sacred books of the Hindus

The Laws of Manu state, "(the king) should carefully compel Vaisyas and Sudras to perform the work (prescribed) for them; for if these two (castes) swerved from their duties, they would throw this (whole) world into confusion." Chap. VIII: 418.

The jajmani system receives its greatest support from the Hindu Sacred Books. The organizers of the Caste-occupational system realized that "the protection of life......must involve the maintenance of a peaceful order, as a condition, if man is to live either securely or well," (page 187, "Study of the Principles of Politics,"—Catlin). And in order to prevent selfish men from throwing "the (whole) world into confusion" the writers of the Sacred Books of the Hindus compiled their beliefs, giving in detail the responsibilities incumbent on all men.

In reference to the occupational duties of mankind, they may be listed as follows:

(1) Man's position in the Universe.

"Of created beings the most excellent are said to be those which are animated; of the animated those which subsist by intelligence; of the intelligent, mankind; and of men, the Brahmanas." Manu I:96.

(2) Men's duties in the Universe.

God assigned separate duties and occupations to men.* Their duties are:

---

*See page xxiv

"5. For a Brahmana, to teach (the Veda);
6. For a Kshatriya, constant practice in arms;
7. For a Vaisya, the tending of cattle;
8. For a Sudra, to serve the twice-born;
9. For all the twice-born, to sacrifice and to study (the Veda).
10. Again, their modes of livelihood are;
11. For a Brahmana, to sacrifice for others and to receive alms;
12. For a Kshatriya, to protect the world (and receive due reward, in form of taxes);
13. For a Vaisya, tillage, keeping cows (and other cattle), traffic, lending money upon interest, and growing seeds:
14. For a Sudra, all branches of art (such as painting and the other five arts);
15. In times of distress, each caste may follow the occupation of that next (below) to it in rank."

(Chapter III "The Institutes of Vishnu, Vol. VIII Sacred Books of the East.")

"The duties of the four castes (varna) in times of distress have thus been declared, and if they perform them well, they will reach the most blessed state." (Manu X:130).

(3) Man's highest goal in the Universe.

The most excellent of Brahmanas are:

"Those learned (in the Veda); of the learned, those who recognize (the necessity and the manner of performing the prescribed duties); of those who possess this knowledge, those who perform them; of the performers, those who know the Brahman (God)". (Manu 1:97.)

a. Not attained by those "given to the acquisition of wealth and to the gratification of their desires".

"The knowledge of the sacred law is prescribed for those who are not given to the acquisition of wealth and to the gratification of their desires; to those who seek the knowledge of the sacred law the supreme authority is the revelation (Sruti.)" (Manu I: 13).

b. Not attained by those "who depart from the rule of conduct":

"A Brahmana who departs from the rule of conduct, does not reap the fruit of the Veda, but he who duly follows it, will obtain the full reward." (Manu I:109.)

c. Not laudable "to act solely from a desire for rewards".

"To act solely from a desire for rewards is not laudable, yet an exemption from that desire is not (to be found) in this (world); for on (that) desire is grounded the study of the Veda and the performance of the actions, prescribed by the Veda." (Manu II:2.)

d. Attained by well-balanced development:

"(Some declare that) the chief good consists in (the acquisition of) spiritual merit and wealth, (others place it) in (the gratification of) desire and (the acquisition of) wealth, (others) in (the acquisition of) spiritual merit alone, and (others say that the acquisition of) wealth alone is the chief good here (below); but the (correct) decision is that it consists of the aggregate of (those) three." (Manu II:224.)

e. Attained by low castes through faithful performance of tasks in this world, thereby attaining a higher caste in the next life.

"But to serve Brahmanas (who are) learned in the Vedas, householders and famous (for virtue) is the highest duty of a Sudra, which leads to beatitude.

"(A Sudra who is) pure, the servant of his betters, gentle in his speech, and free from pride, and always seeks a refuge with Brahmanas, attains (in his next life) a higher caste." (Manu IX: 334, 335.)

By serving Brahmans, Sudras gain all their ends. Whatever else they may do will bear them no fruit.

(4) The place of man who has failed to perform his occupational duties.*

The men of the different caste divisions will migrate into despicable bodies if they fail to perform their duties.†

---

*See pages xviii-xix

†See page xxv

D. Law of the State

The Hindu Jajmani System has been further strengthened by the law of the State, as already illustrated in the Introduction. Sir Henry Sumner Maine states, "I shall have to advert to the curious circumstance that the influence of thesc Brahmanical theories upon law has been rather increased than otherwise by the British dominion." (page 20 "Village Communities in the East and West.")

William Adam in "The Law and Custom of Slavery in British India" gives a review of the development of English Law Courts in India which develops the statement made by Sir Henry Sumner Maine.

> "An extensive territory by cession or conquest had through the agency of the East India Company, become subject to the crown and sovereignty of Great Britain. A primary and essential duty of every just government towards its subjects is that of publishing and enforcing an equitable system of law, adapted to their actual condition and circumstances, and calculated to protect them in the secure enjoyment of their rights, natural and acquired. In the view of this obligation, by various statutes in the reign of George III, a supreme court of judicature, consisting of a chief justice and three other judges was established at Calcutta, and the benefit of the laws of England, as far as applicable to India, was extended by the legislature to all persons residing within the town of Calcutta, and subsequently to all British subjects, natives of Great Britain, or their descendants, resident in India or elsewhere within the limits of the East India Company's exclusive trade. But the laws of England were justly deemed inapplicable to the native population who, whether Mohammedans or Hindus, were previously in possession of their respective written laws, under which they had acquired property by descent, purchase, gift, and other modes, and which they had been educated and habituated to regard and venerate as sacred. There was accordingly in the statutes above mentioned, a reservation of the laws and usages of the native inhabitants of Calcutta in cases of 'inheritance and succession to lands, rents,

and goods, and all matters of contract and dealing between party and party, as well as the rights and authorities of fathers and masters of families'; that is, in all such cases, native laws and usages were to be recognized and maintained. In 1772, the laws and usages of the native inhabitants of the provinces were as distinctly recognized. In that year, a plan for the administration of justice in the provinces was adopted, and it was provided 'that in all suits regarding inheritance, marriage, caste, and other religious usages or institutions, the laws of the *Koran* with respect to Mohammedans, and those of the Shaster with respect to Gentoos, shall be invariably adhered to. On all such occasions the Moulavies' (interpreters of Mohammedan Law) 'or Brahmins' (interpreters of Hindu law) 'shall respectively attend to expound the law, and they shall sign the report, and, assist in passing the decree.' Instead of the judicial plan of 1772, a more comprehensive system of law and regulation was established by the Marquis Cornwallis in 1793, and in that system also the following rule was laid down for preserving to the natives their own laws and usages; 'In suits regarding succession, inheritance, marriage, and caste, and all religious usages and institutions, the Mohammedan laws with respect to Mohammedans, and the Hindu laws with regard to Hindus, are to be considered the general rules by which the judges are to form their decision.' This, then, was an original and has always continued to be a primary, rule of British law in India; and if the fundamental principle of all civil laws is, that they ought to be 'suitable to the genius of the people' subject to their authority and operation, the wisdom, the justice, and the humanity of adopting and adhering to it, must be pronounced equally honourable to the British nation and government, and conducive to the protection and contentment of the natives of India." (pages 24-26).

The following statement on the treatment of Hindu law under Mohammedan dominion is significant.

"Until the recognition of Hindu civil law by the British Government in 1772, that law had no legal force or obligation wherever the authority of the Mohammedan government extended, during a preceding period of from 700 to 750 years. By this it is not meant to be affirmed that Hindus, during that period, under the Mohammedan government, did not practically observe their own laws of succession and inheritance, marriage and caste, and even of slavery; but that those laws were not recognized and enforced by the Mohammedan government, and that the only law recognized and enforced by that government, was the law of Islam. This is a necessary consequence of the spirit and principle of the Mohammedan religion, and of all Mohammedan governments. By the Mohammedan law a foreign province or country becomes annexed to the Mohammedan dominions by the mere act of conquest and the exercise of even a part of the law of Islam in it; and to establish the law of Islam within the Mohammedan dominions is mandatory on Mohammedan rulers, and not optional to them. Even questions of inheritance among non-Moslem subjects are not left to the decision of any other than a Moslem tribunal, but must be decided according to the Mohammedan law, and by Moslem judges, for every judge must be a Moslem. During the whole period of the Mohammedan history in India, though Hindus were employed in the highest offices of trust and emolument, yet a Hindu judge was never heard of, and assuredly no Mohammedan Kazi could every have been found to administer the civil laws of the Hindus. It follows that the Hindu law, including the law of slavery, however, it may have been reverenced and observed by the Hindus themselves, or tolerated by the more enlightened Mohammedan princes, had no force or obligation during the whole period of the Mohammedan rule, and that it was in every legal sense a dead letter until it was re-enacted by the British Government in 1772, and confirmed by the system of law and regulation promulgated in 1793. Up to the former of these periods, the Hindu law had no vitality. It could not be pleaded in any court of justice. It could not form the ground of any judicial decision. It was legally as if it had never been." (pages 30-31)

As illustrative of the manner in which English judges consulted Brahmans, we have in the case of Radha Kishen and others, Appellants *vs.* Sham Serma, Ram Deb Serma, Pulta Ram Sahoo, Kishen Sahoo, and others, Respondents, an action which was brought in "the Zillah Court of Tipperah, on the 13th of November, 1818, by the appellants, who are Brahmans, to establish their right to officiate as Purohits, or priests, to 31 families of Sahoos, who inhabit, the village of Chapulpara. The suit was laid at 505 Rupees the annual amount of fees."

In the court record we find the following statement:

"Previously to the admission of the special appeal, the Court put the following questions to their pundits: 1st, is a Jajman authorized, under any circumstances, to discard a faultless Purohit, whether he be a family Purohit, or one appointed by the Jajman? 2nd, if a Jajman discharge a faultless Purohit, and pay the fine, must he afterwards employ the same Purohit or not?"

The pundits gave the following answers:

"Answer 1st, "A Jajman has no power to discharge a Purohit whether he be a family Purohit, or one appointed by himself, if the Purohit be without fault, and labour under no disqualifications: for it is laid down in the Shaster, that a Jajman, who discards a faultless Purohit is punishable by fine. A faultless Purohit, therefore, he cannot discard."

"Authority, Munnoo in the 'Vivada Bhungarnuba', 'Vivada Chintamunee', and other tracts: 'If a Jajman discard a Purohit who is faultless, and capable of performing the duty of Purohit, or if a Purohit discharge a faultless Jajman, he is liable to fine of 100 puns'."

"Answer 2nd: 'If a Jajman discard a faultless Purohit, and pay the fine due for that offence, it is necessary for him to perform prayushchitta (atonement), and to re-appoint the Purohit; for a Ritwig and Purohit are equal, and it is incumbent on them, that they, in all matters laid down in the Shaster, be careful to do everything for the advantage of their Jajmans, and to remove harm from them; if any discharge a Purohit, who should be looked upon as father, mother and gooroo, he is guilty of such a crime, as excludes him from eating and drinking with his tribe in this world, and will cause him to be hereafter born in the body of a rakhis, or demon. This crime is called Oopupatuk. Moreover, it is necessary to serve such a person (a Purohit) as a father or mother; and the person who takes away (or withholds) the dukshina, or other gifts usually given by Jajmans, which are the means of subsistence of Brahmins, is guilty of a serious offence. Let the person

> who discards his Purohit, having paid the fine to the Raja, and made the atonement (prayushchitta) laid down in the Shaster in retribution for that offence, again appoint the Purohit to his office. This is enjoined by the Shaster. It is also incumbent on the Raja to levy the fine from any of his subjects who act contrary to his duty, and to compel him to keep to his duty (dhurum). The Raja is culpable, if he do not take notice of such thing."

This is followed by thirteen quotations taken by the Pundits from various Sacred Books of the Hindus. ("Bengal Sudder Reports 1812-1819" by W. H. MacNaghten, pages 332-340.)

The majority of cases in the Law Reports deal with "birt Jajmani" and "birt Mahabrahmani" as referring to the relationship of the hereditary priest, the "purohit" to his client, the "jajman." Mr. Brij Behari Lal, Judge of the Small Cause Court of Allahabad, under date of April 21, 1932 confirms this observation.

> "Mostly, the rulings are about the rights of priests, 'Pragwals,' (those who sit on the banks of the Ganges and take alms),' Gayawals' (those who officiate at Gaya at 'Shradh' ceremonies), 'Mahabrahmins' (those who officiate at funeral ceremonies). Village carpenters, Dhunas, Manihars, Kumhars, etc. are poor people, and are not likely to take the question of their rights to High Courts. They get small doolefuls of grain for service, either at harvest time, or have their service tenure tenancy land. Their rights in some villages are defined in the *Wajib-ul-arz* of the village. Morcover their dues are dependent on the performance of the specific service...., If their rights are taken away by somebody the aggrieved seeks help from landlords, and the village who require his services. If they back him well and good, the person defeated takes it sportingly, if the village people accept the new man, the old man retires sulkily.
>
> "As to service tenure tenancy, as long as the man performs the duties he enjoys generation after generation, widows being allowed to import persons for the due performance of that duty, if there is no direct male issue."

Some of the recent court decisions bring out clearly the rights of this system.

The right is considered by the Hindu Law as immovable property.

> "In English Treaties on Inheritance S 206, Para. 26, the rule is quoted as follows:
>
> 'The right of performing religious ceremonies of certain classes of people as Purohit, is by custom considered analogous to real property. The ancestral priest, that is, he who has been honoured by former generations with employment of officiating priest, and the priest appointed by the party himself, cannot be discarded without good and sufficient cause; but there is no legal authority for establishing the right of the heirs to officiate. The male heir of an hereditary purohit is, however, by custom considered entitled thereto, but not the heirs of an appointed priest. A female cannot succeed to such right and perform the ceremonies by a substitute, because she can appoint a substitute only for worldly affairs, not for solemn acts for the performance of which she herself is disqualified. Several male heirs share the fees according to their respective portions, and if they have divided the jajmans among them, each one will take the fees from his respective jajmans.'
>
> "On a view of the authorities quoted above we have come to the conclusion that under Hindu Law the right to receive offerings from jajmans is considered as immovable property and, therefore, capable, of passing by inheritance to the heirs of the persons in enjoyment of such rights and is, therefore, divisible among the heirs."
>
> (All-India Reporter, 1930 (Oudh) page 257)

Alienation of rights under certain conditions is not opposed to the principles of Hindu law.

> "The right to worship and its remuneration is ordinarily inalienable but when as here the alienation is to a member of the family or to a Brahman of the same caste as the alienor and equally competent to perform the worship, it cannot be said to be opposed to the principles of Hindu Law or public policy."

"It is said that the general principle is that *Vritties* (jajmani rights) are alienable to suitable persons unless a local custom to the contrary or some prohibition by the founder can be proved.

"*Vritties* may be alienated in special cases and under special conditions provided that such alienations can be supported by local usage and custom." (The Indian Law Reports, Vol. XXXIX, Bombay Series, page 26)

The rights of women to inherit jajmani rights is well described in the Madras Law Journal.

"The question whether sex is a disqualification to inherit must be decided with reference to the particular facts of each case, the nature of the functions to be performed by the office holder, the amount of remuneration, whether it leaves a surplus or not, and other similar matters." (Madras Law Journal., Vol. 26, page 315).

SECTION III

Disintegrating Factors in the Hindu Jajmani System

1. The Hindu Jajmani System is a disintegrated form of the ancient Village Commune.

The Hindu Jajmani System as it stands today in Karimpur is ancient in that it recognizes the claims of the different occupational groups to a share of the earnings of the village as a whole, but is not ancient in its detailed form as described in the preceding pages. Radhakamal Mukerjee in "Democracies of the East" points out that in the primitive Dravidian society "the tribes are subdivided and grouped into village communities, each under a headman, who allots the land within the village area, and settles any disputes as to the location of any family; there is a hierarchy of village officers, who look after tribal morality and the equable distribution of land; there is an elaborate establishment of lots or holdings for the headman, the priest, the deputy or accountant, and a staff of artisans and employees." (page 200)

> "Among the Santals there existed or still exists an actual custom by which they give up all their lands, excepting their house sites at the end of the Santal year, and only resume individual possession after getting the sanction of the *panchayat*. Again, the periodical distribution of holdings held by non-privileged families and settlers and a regulation of rights in the common forest or sacred grove, which still remains intact in Chota Nagpur and Coorg, can still be traced. Everywhere among the Dravidian peoples, plots of land are set apart from the common village settlements for village officers, artisans, and servants, and this

has affected the land distribution especially of Madras, Bombay, and the Central Provinces." (Ibid, page 201.)

The intermingling of Dravidian patterns of village economic organization with those of the Aryan invaders is described by Mukerjee as follows:

"It is very probable that the rice-growing races of the South, among whom the institution of the communal holding of land with periodical redistribution of the fields is inherent, took to Northern India (where Karimpur is located) the custom of communal ownership along with the *panchayat,* the appointment of which was the effect of the system of shifting tenures. Wheat and barley are associated with individualistic as rice with communalistic organization of agricultural society. Wheat cultivation came first to Northern India with the Aryan stocks, with whom land was held as the family property. They did not live in contiguous huts like those of the Dravidians, but the whole family lived together in their own homestead. As both these principal crops have grown together ideas of indiivdual and communal proprietory rights have intermingled in the North, though there preponderates here the rule of individual (or family) property in land which distinguishes the *bhaiachara* and *pattidari* systems of tenure. The gradual process of Hinduization, again, implies the supersession of the Dravidian promiscuity by the institution of the joint family, and thus the development of family rights in many places has eclipsed the old communal customs in the *ryotwari* villages of the South." (Ibid, page 203.)

"All the *watan* lands and the various privileges and dignities associated with them constituted a family property which was capable of descending to a number of heirs jointly. Further, in each village there grew up a staff of officials, artisans, and employees who became hereditary and served the village, not for payment by the job (such a thing, of course, was unknown) but for a regular remuneration, paid in kind, chiefly by a fixed share in the harvest." (Ibid, page 205.)

Later, "conquest or usurpation, or Mohammedan dominion and grant, introduced many grantees and other superior holders of estates whose successors remain to this day. It is very significant, however, that the Mohammedan land-holding villages and tribes in Northern India generally follow the custom of family land-holding. The Mohammedan law of inheritance is not much adhered to, the joint-family system is observed." (Ibid, page 205.)

Thus we find that the Hindu Jajmani System in its purest form was a corruption of the ancient system of "the custom of communal ownership" directed by the *panchayat*.

2. The British system of Government and Law.

Mukerjee writes, "The Anglo-Indian land revenue system is the most recent of the forces of disintegration, but has only eclipsed, not superseded, the strength of the village community and of its assembly. The policy of direct relations with the individual *ryots* (farmers) in matters of land revenue—a system which has been long in force under the British aegis in Madras and Bombay, and which is tending to substitute itself for the old joint proprietory *ryots* in the United Provinces—has worked as much mischief as legislation and administration on an individualistic basis, or the establishment of local civil and criminal courts, but has not entirely suppressed communal interests and the regular village system, which is still rendering useful service. The Board of Revenue, Madras, making a last protest against the introduction of the *Ryotwari* Settlement, which in their opinion threatened to break up the community of interest on which the village system depends, once remarked: 'To dissolve this unity of interest and common stock of labour by requiring each to take, instead of a share he possessed and owned, a defined part of the whole land of the village, would not be very different from dissolving a joint-stock company in England, and requiring each proprietor to trade upon his own portion of it, in order that it may be separately taxed.' But the dissolution has continued since in the intererests of a bureaucratic system of revenue collection and management, though the village system, notwithstanding, still retains its unity. Throughout the country the village assemblies are still administering village affairs, finance and justice. Neither Mauryan bureaucracy, nor Mohammedan inroads, neither the centralized administration of Akbar or of Aurangzeb, nor the modern British *ryotwari* or permanent settlement, have

> obliterated the traditional rights of the village communities as described in the *Arthasastra* or the *Sukraniti*, though the tendencies of British rule have been most disintegrating and disruptive so far as the village system is concerned." (Ibid, page 206-207.)

Sir Henry Sumner Maine explains the actions of the British as follows:

> "The Village-Community did not emerge into clear light very early in the history of our conquest and government. Although this peculiar group is referred to in Manu, the English found little to guide them to its great importance in the Brahmanical codified law of the Hindoos which they first examined. Perhaps in the large space assigned in that law to joint-property and partitions they might have found a hint of the truth, if the great province in which they were first called upon to practice administration on a large scale, Lower Bengal or Bengal proper, had not happened to be the exact part of India in which, from causes not yet fully determined, the village system had fallen into great decay. The assumption which the English first made was one which they inherited from their Mohammedan predecessors. It was, that all the soil belonged in absolute property to the sovereign, and that all private property in land existed by his sufferance." (Page 104 "Village Communities in the East and West".)

The British-India Government not only recognizes the individual as having rights in land, but likewise in the law courts. This has done much to weaken the power of the *Panchayat* in the village and to strengthen the powerful individual. Illustrations of this fact have already been given in the discussion under the heading of village elders. On the other hand, there is a danger that the Council of Elders, no longer engaged in its ancient functions, may work at cross purposes to those of the Central Government Officers. Shortly before our first contact with the village, a water-bearer girl of sixteen years of age committed suicide by jumping into a well. The District police officers came in to investigate. They heard rumours as to the cause of the act, namely that one of the leading Brahmans in the village had violated her. In order to protect herself and the man, the girl had committed suicide. The police officers instructed the local elders to look into the matter and render help to them in the case. It was referred to them not as a body having power, but one having influence. The result was negative as far as justice was coneerned. In fact, justice was subverted because steps were taken by the elders to protect the Brahman in ways not legal. Had a similar case occurred under the old village regime, with the *Panchayat* as highest authority, the elders would have recognized their responsibilities and the offender would have been punished—probably, however, not severely cnough to meet modern conceptions of punishment.

Dr. Sanderson states that, "Thc studies of villages made by Dr. Slaters's students seem to indicate that, at least in southern India, wherever the *panchayats* have disappeared and the village affairs are merely administered by the headman and accountant, the village solidarity has been lost and the general cultural level of the village has been distinctly lowered." ("The Rural Community," pages 337, 338.)

Another disintegrating factor in the Hindu Jajmani System is the introduction of a free Government School system, with its staff of trained teachers drawn from every caste and religion. The Karimpur school had two school teachers, one a rice grower (of the Sudra division) and the other a Kyasth (accountant), neither being of the caste established by the Hindu system as those fit to teach. When arguing with some parents about their refusal to permit their children to attend school along with sweepers, we pointed out that if sweepers were not supposed to learn, how could they justify having their children taught by a rice grower. They quickly retorted, "We are not responsible for that. Government apppointed him teacher." No protest had been registered against his being a teacher, and unconsciously new conceptions of those who are fit to teach were being brought into the minds of the children—conceptions quite different from those held by their forefathers.

3. Functional Changes.

Functional change does not necessarily mean disintegration, since the Laws of Manu provided for changes of function downwards in the caste scale "in times of distress." But every change in function means an upset in equilibrium. And the nice balance which has been secured through a careful division oflabour is disturbed. Each such disturbance tends to introduce doubt as to the infallibility of the Hindu Jajmani System, and each such doubt must be considered a factor of disintegration.

Reference has already been made to the fact that about the 11th Century the Rajputs replaced the Kshatriyas* in performing the function of warriors for the Hindu Jajmani System. The Kshatriyas had to shift as best they could within the laws of right action.

The Brahman, bard, barber, water-bearer, and washerman in refusing to serve some of their fellow Hindu castes on the grounds that they are untouchable are contributing to the disintegration of their own religious system. Sir P. C. Ray wrote:

> "A house divided against itself cannot stand. The backward classes are flesh of our flesh and bone of our bone and it is the bounden duty of our men of light and leading to extend to them

*See pages 26 ffg.

the right hand of fellowship and lift them up from the quagmire of degradation and despondency." (The *Leader* of Allahabad, November 2, 1930.)

It is small wonder that Christian and Mohammedan missionaries have been successful in gaining converts from among the low caste groups. These groups cannot get service from their so-called brothers in the Hindu faith. Why not join an organization that will give them the full rights of brotherhood?

It has already been pointed out that with the exception of the barber and washerman, who are constantly kept busy, all castes engage in a certain amount of agriculture. According to the traditions, the vegetable growers and rice growers were the intensive farmers. Gradually other castes are doing their own farming, both intensive and extensive. The vegetable growers and rice growers are thus left without a special function to perform for the village community. It is not a cause of anxiety to them because they can be independent with their knowledge of agricultural methods. But the Hindu Jajmani System with its specially assigned duties cannot mean the same to them as it did when they were the only ones with special agricultural skill.

A similar situation is arising in reference to shepherds and cattle raisers. As all castes engage in agriculture they need oxen to help them. And a growing desire for milk, apart from the religious values, encourages farmers to keep cows and buffaloes. The poorer villagers keep goats. Hence we find more and more shepherds and cattle raisers becoming agriculturists. The Ahirs (cattle raisers) in Mainpuri District are so successful with their agriculture that they have become powerful political leaders in the District. They contributed enough for, and continue to maintain, a first class High School at Shikohabad, just 32 miles distance from Mainpuri—our headquarters. Groups like these, furnish excellent support for the introduction of new political and social ideas, because under the Hindu Jajmani System they gain very little, whereas apart from it they can attain to power equivalent to that of any of the more favoured Twice-Born.

Another group that does not form an essential part of the Hindu Jajmani System are the Vaisyas, who are altogether absent in Karimpur. Sir Henry Sumner Maine confirms this observation. "It is a remarkable fact that certain callings, extremely respectable and lucrative, do not appear in India to constitute those who follow them, members of the village-community. Eminent officials have assured me that, so far as their experience extends, the grain dealer (Vaisya) is never a hereditary trader incorporated with the village group." (page 126, "Village Communities in the East and West"). It is of interest to note that the Vaisyas who have so little share in the Hindu Jajmani System are likewise active in the present political disturbances. Mr. Gandhi is a member of this caste and observers of the Home-Rule movement in the United Provinces have often called it a Vaisya movement.

Other disruptive factors in function are coming in through the part that competition with the outside world is playing in the life of the village people. The goldsmiths are in part being replaced by city competition. Woolen mufflers, cakes, and blankets made in Italy are replacing those made from home-spun wool formerly supplied by the shepherd; the potters find a ready market for dung fuel cakes which would otherwise be locally consumed; aluminum vessels and lanterns made in Germany and the U. S. A. are replacing vessels and lamps formerly made in the village or nearby; cash payment for services in towns has led to the introduction of cash payments in the village; numerous outsiders sell things to the villagers but do not themselves constitute a part of the Jajmani System; and finally, powerful jajmans themselves are tempted by external opportunities, as is illustrated by the following incident.

The various "kam karnewalas" of a nearby village had made their annual payments of grain due to their jajman on advances made. His own crops were good and his granaries were full. The village people settled back with the assurance of an adequate grain supply to meet their winter needs. Crop failures in other parts of the world had caused prices to rise and the jajman saw a chance to make big profits. He accordingly decided to sell his grain. He began loading his carts and word was quickly passed round the village as to what was going to happen to their winter supply of grain. They came to their jajman from all sides and pleaded with him to consider his duty to his "kam karnewalas." But to no avail. The oxen were yoked to the carts and started for the grain market. The villagers decided that the time for action had come. They unyoked the carts, brought a scale and weighed out the grain, distributing it to each of the "kam karnewalas" as required for their winter needs. A careful record was kept and when the grain was all distributed, the record was given to the jajman. He was furious and went at once to the District police. All the men in the village were arrested. Although the law was on the side of the jajman, the Superintendent of Police sympathized with the villagers and they were sent away with a warning. If many jajmans treated their "kam karnewalas" in this way the Hindu Jajmani System would soon break down. This incident is not of general occurrence, but indicates another of the ways in which disintegrating factors are at work in the Hindu Jajmani System.

Modern reform movements of both a political and religious nature are introducing elements of discontent in the thinking of village "kam karnewalas". One vegetable grower's father now looks forward to the day when his son may have a "white collar" job and be spared the drudgery of agriculture. His forefathers would never have dared to think such a thought. Sweepers, the lowest of the low, through accepting Christianity, look forward to their sons and daughters becoming professional people. They no longer cower before their jajmans. Several years ago there was a misunderstanding between a sweeper and one of his Brahman jajmans. Words led to blows and the participants were quickly joined by sympathizers. Among others, the Brahman jajman received several injuries. Later in the course of a meeting of the *panchayat*, one of the village elders said to the writer, "If these sweepers had not become Christians, they would never have dared to strike a Brahman." Thus the disintegrating factors are at work today in Karimpur.

In conclusion, an analysis of the earnings from the jajmani caste occupations in Karimpur, reveals economic weakness in the system in its insufficient provision for its "kam karnewalas". (See Table II). Forty-four families of menial castes,—the vegetable grower, rice grower, water-bearer, shepherd, potter, tradesman and bangle-seller are altogether unprovided for by the system. The industry of the individual rather than the interest of the community plays the largest part in the lives of these people. This lack of community accommodation constitutes a

TABLE II

Analysis of Earnings from Jajmani Caste Occupations in Karimpur.

Caste of Kam Karnewala	Families			Karimpur Brahman's estimate of economic status of each Jajmani caste occupation			Entire income from occupation		Income from occupation in Karimpur supplemented by agriculture			Income from occupation in Karimpur and elsewhere supplemented by agriculture	
									Bulk of earnings			Bulk of earnings	
	Total Number	Dependent on Jajmani system	Independent of Jajmani System	Good	Fair	Poor	In Karimpur	with other villages	from occupation	from agriculture	from Aglabour	from occupation	from agriculture
Brahman ...	41	3	38	3	...	...	...	1	...	1	...	...	1
Bard ...	2	2	...	...	...	2	...	...	...	2	...	...	...
Accountant ...	1	...	1	...	...	...	...	...	...	...	...	...	...
Goldsmith ...	2	2	...	2	...	...	...	2	...	...	...	...	...
Florist ...	1	1	...	1	...	...	...	...	...	...	...	...	1
Vegetable grower ...	26	...	26	...	...	...	...	...	...	...	...	...	...
Rice grower ...	1	...	1	...	...	...	...	...	...	...	...	...	...
Carpenter-iron-worker ...	8	3	...	4	3	1	...	...	7*	...	...	1	...

Barber ...	1	1	...	1	...	...	1	...	...	...	...	...	...
Water-bearer ...	19	11	8	...	2	9	...	...	1	5	5	...	...
Shepherd ...	6	2	4	...	...	2	...	...	2	...	...	...	...
Grain parcher ...	1	1	...	...	1	...	...	...	...	1	...	...	...
Seamster ...	5	5	...	1	4	...	...	5	...	...	...	...	...
Potter ...	3	3	...	2	...	...	...	3	...	...	...	...	...
Tradesman ...	3	1	2	...	...	...	...	1	...	...	...	...	...
Oil presser ...	4	4	...	...	...	4	...	...	...	...	...	4	...
Washerman ...	1	1	...	...	1	...	...	1	...	...	...	...	...
Mat-maker ...	7	7	...	...	...	7	...	...	...	4	3	...	...
Leather worker ...	8	8	...	...	...	8	...	...	...	...	8	...	...
Sweeper ...	8	8	...	1	...	7	...	...	...	...	...	8	...
Faqir ...	8	8	...	...	...	8	...	...	...	...	...	2	6
Bangle-seller ...	2	1	1	1	...	...	...	...	...	...	...	1	...
Cotton carder ...	1	1	...	...	...	1	...	...	...	...	...	...	1
Dancing girl ...	2	2	...	...	...	2	...	...	...	...	...	2	...
Total ...	161	80	81	16	11	51	1	13	10	13	16	18	9

*With help of religious fairs

definite disintegrating faetor in the life of the jajmani system in Karimpur.

According to the table we find that out of 161 families who might be potential members of the Hindu Jajmani System with a symmetrical service relationship, only 80 funetion on this basis. Thirty-eight Brahman families have no share in priestly duties beeause 3 can adequately meet the needs of the eommunity. 1 aeeountant is employed by the government; 26 vegetable growers and 1 rice grower perform the traditional work of agrieulture whieh is no longer a speeialized service required by the eommunity; 8 water-bearers have not established fixed relationships because the 11 other water-bearer families are suffieient to meet the village needs; 4 shepherds have had to engage in agrieulture beeause there is no eneouragement for them to remain shepherds; 2 tradesmen await opportunities for purchases and sales whenever occasion may arise; and 1 bangle seller, who is not popular with the villagers, makes his living by selling bracelets in nearby villages. The relation of these 81 families in the village to the other 80 is on an asymmetrieal serviee basis. They are served, but do not serve.

In spite of its various eompensations and rights, Karimpur does not treat its "kam karnewalas" very well. Aeeording to the judgment of a prosperous Brahman in the village, only 16, or 20.5 per eent, enjoy a good eeonomic status in the village, and 11 or 14.1 per cent enjoy a fair eeonomie status, whereas 51, or 65.4 per cent have a poor eeonomic status.

Of the 80 families only 14 draw their entire income from their oeeupation, together with the privileges they enjoy in the matter of keeping animals—the potters and washerman with their donkeys, and their selling of dung cakes, the sweepers with their pigs, and the dancing girl with her goats. Of the 14, all but one have to work for other villages besides Karimpur in order to gain their livelihood. The remaining 66 families have to supplement their earnings with agriculture. Of these 66, 18 earn more from their occupational work than from agriculture, whereas 38 earn more from agriculture. The other ten, not noted on the table depend on other sources of income. Thirty-nine of the 66 perform their ocupational work and agriculture within the village boundaries. Twenty-seven have to find extra opportunities for work from nearby villages.

SECTION IV

Evaluation of the Hindu Jajmani System

IN evaluating the Hindu Jajmani System, one is conscious of a conflict between group and community concepts on one hand and individualistic concepts on the other. And one is torn between an acceptance of the social unity created by a social structure such as caste, and an acceptance of individualism which forms such an uncertain basis for social solidarity. It will be well, therefore, before considering conclusions, to review in part the philosophy underlying each concept. In this section, we will consider the advantages and disadvantages of a social pattern like the Hindu Jajmani System in relation to the nation, the community, the functional group and the individual. In presenting these advantages and disadvantages, the writer has felt free to draw on various authors who have studied the philosophy underlying individualism and group relationships.

1. The Jajmani System in relation to the nation.

(*a*) *Advantages*

The interrelation of services in Karimpur has served to correlate the activities of the residents of the community in a complete social unit. In becoming a strong social unit with an individuality of its own, the community has rendered its greatest service to the nation, as conceived by the Easterner. Mukerjee says, "we have myriads of semi-independent local or non-local bodies having particulate jurisdictions, which overlap and interlock, intersect and outreach—which are not a series of concentric circles as in the west, each enveloping the other till it is absorbed by the all-embracing State. Thus in the East we may more appropriately define politics to be the search for social unity rather than sovereignty; law is more the custom and tradition of an organization of co-operating social functions than the fiat of the State. While the West tends to adopt a sort of mystic monism as the true path of political thought and activity, recognizing no natural limits of political administration, the East draws its inspiration from the shifting variety of a teeming multiplicity." (Democracies of the East, Page 24.)

(*b*) *Disadvantages*

This system of autonomous village social organization causes a conflict with centralization of power and national loyalties. As Dr Sanderson states, "The peasant of the village community had no keen sense of nationality; his loyalty was first to his kindred and to his community." (Sanderson, "The Rural Community", page 567.)

2. The Jajmani system in relation to the village community.

(*a*) *Advantages*

The strength of the Empire in India is reflected in the strength of the communities, because "federalism is the essence of social grouping in the East". (Mukerjee, "Democracies of the East", page 357.) In India we find a

"communal-federal tradition." "The East throughout has preserved the vitality of small local groups, giving opportunity to the humblest citizens organized in guilds, village communities, and communal assemblies for continuous political activity even in daily toil, economic functioning, or social intercourse. Occupational or functional representation has been the foundation on which the whole fabric of indigenous popular government in the East has rested; and there has emerged out of the voluntary co-operation of myriad groups the common idea, the collective will of the people, in which majority and minority ideas are closely interwoven, (Mukerjee, Ibid, page 346.)

Dr. Sanderson writes, "It is the strong organization of the village community for its own economic and social purposes, without political bias, which made the village community in India so seemingly immortal." (Dwight Sanderson, "The Rural Community", page 360.)

Dr. Wilson writes, "For caste is a conservative shelter to which, being poor, the individual Indian can retreat that he may be fed and clothed. It follows that in the normal Indian village there are no beggars, no paupers, and there is no need of institutions for blind or deaf. All these are cared for by their kindred and everyone is fed. By the normal process of Indian village life the blind and lame are fed and sheltered, the unemployed are welcomed." (Publication of the American Sociological Society, Vol. 25, No. 4, page 54. Warren H. Wilson.)

"The village unit is a subsistence unit into which the people can retreat when want or scarcity is felt, and within which the social bonds, drawn ever tighter, bind up in obligations and secure against want each member of the village community." "There is something in the Indian rural economy that makes poverty and hard work bearable. I cannot help but think that poverty sheltered by society is different from the poverty of those exploited by economic organization of mankind." "To the Indian villager economy is not the way of life, but the social organization and the inherited toil on their overpopulated land." "The villages are—except for the effect of natural disasters—immortal. The families prefer their own continuance to the independence of their individual members. The whole structure of village society is calculated to enable the people to retreat into sociological defense away from the attacks of economic forces. These economic assailants are organized in two battalions. The one is the city, considered as a cluster, or corps, of modern industries, factories, banks, brokers, financiers. The other economic battalion is the government." (Ibid, pages 56, 58, 59, 60.)

The Hindu Jajmani System gives "a satisfactory life of the local group (which) is possible only when there is a certain unity of purpose among its institutions representing the different interests of its people." (Sanderson "The Rural Community", page 475.) " 'The will to will the common will' is the core of the community." (Sanderson, Ibid, page 594.) The Hindu Jajmani System has an integration which is an embryonic form of what Dr. Sanderson considers essential to the modern rural cmmunity. "Physical, economic, psycholcgical, and social forces are all bringing about the integration of the rural community around a common centre of the interests of those living within an area which can support the institutions desired. If civilization is to advance and the increasing desires of humanity are to be satisfied, such an integration is inevitable. (Ibid, page 476), and the proper emphasis "Business will not be so largely the centre of the field of attention as it now is, but will take its rightful place as a means to an end, the end being the highest welfare of the community." (Ibid, page 567.)

The Jajmani System has developed through social solidarity a social heritage which "includes, besides habitation, tools and weapons, language, institutions, and traditions, which register racial gains." Through "geographical segregation" it has encouraged "inbreeding" and brought "about stability of type and psychical integration by means of similar responses." (Radhakamal Mukerjee, "Regional Sociology", page 218.) "This community of interest is a phase of symbiosis or commensalism based not merely upon mutual advantage and mutual toleration but also upon strict independence and self-help......All the species which take part in such associations may be said to converge towards a common centre of subsistence, and this community of habitat leads to similar convergence of character. In human groups we have similarities of modes of behaviour arising similarly under the stimulus of a common region." (Mukerjee, Ibid, pages 220-221.)

In reference to social control the Jajmani system meets the requirements of Professor Ross' five canons:

"(1) Each increment of social interference should bring more benefit to persons as members of society than it entails inconvenience to persons as individuals." This gain comes to the members of the Jajmani system.

"(2) Social interference should not lightly excite against itself the passion for liberty." The Panchayat seems unconsciously to recognize this principle. "The duty which the headman and the panchayat felt in any case submitted to them seems primarily to have been rather to find a means for composing the differences and satisfying both parties than to award a decree in favour of one and to leave the other an absolute loser." (Sanderson, "The Rural Community", page 342.)

"(3) Social interference should respect the sentiments that are the support of natural order." This is done without effort.

"(4) Social interference should not be so paternal as to check the self-extinction of the morally ill constituted." There is little danger of this is in the Indian village.

"(5) Social interference should not so limit the struggle for existence as to nullify the selective process." The Indian villager does not feel that he is limited by his fixed status although an outside observer may disagree with him. (See pages 419-425, "Social Control" by E. A. Ross.)

"It was the village community which developed those social attitudes of mutual aid, equity, and obligation for the common welfare which form the basis of the moral code and are the dynamic element of the social heritage of most of mankind—The village community has conserved the human values secured through the mutual aid of those who learned how to feed mankind by agriculture—Without the village community man would have been unable to perfect the art of agriculture; he would have been unable to produce and store a surplus of food, which made all other progress possible—The history of the village community exemplifies the strength of the locality group as a means of insuring the common welfare in a relatively isolated environment." (Sanderson, "The Rural Community," pages 433-434.)

(*b*) *Disadvantages*

The Hindu Jajmani System could probably stand as it is in a static world, but the world is dynamic. The Hindu village community has to meet conditions arising from this fact. It cannot withstand the competition of trade from the outside without making some radical adjustments in its own social organization. Human needs are measured in terms of an outside market and community loyalties are broken down. As a matter

of history, Dr. Sanderson shows that "the growth of the cities, providing markets for agricultural produce, and the consequent spread of a money economy and the commercialization of agriculture were important factors in destroying the old self-sufficiency of the village community and in creating new wants and desires among its members......Communication has opened a new world to the village peasant; and once he has 'eaten of the fruit of the tree of knowledge' he is no longer satisfied to be dominated by the customary control of the community, which, he comes to feel, is no longer adapted to meet his needs. His desire for better conditions replaces his reverence for custom." (Sanderson, Ibid, page 422 and page 426,)

Dr. Sanderson further states in reference to the history of the village community that

"we owe little of modern progress to the village community. ......Its decline is chiefly owing to the fact that it lacks any motives or stimuli which impel the development of the individual so that he can think for himself. There is no incentive to abstract thought. The village community lives on a perpetual plane and finds satisfaction in its collective thought........With improved methods and mechanisms for crop production the village system becomes uneconomical and is unable to furnish a standard of life which is satisfying to those who come into contact with a superior culture......It shows the inability of purely customary social control to effect a progiessive adjustment of human association." (Sanderson, Ibid, pages 433-434.)

In its economic isolation, without thorough integration with other communities, the village community suffers from poverty and famine "for there is no means whereby capital may be accumulated and whereby the necessities of life may be transported from one section to another in time of need." (Sanderson, Ibid, page 323.)

The system is weak in that it derives some of its strength from access to waste land. This right of access according to B. H. Baden-Powell, cannot be an unlimited right.

> "The fact is, that for ages past, no idea of the value of *forests*, as such, ever existed. The 'Waste' was looked on as literally *waste;* the Sovereign or the local Chief always had the right to make a grant out of it to any one; and he often reserved large tracts to himself for hunting grounds (called shikargah; and 'ramna'—by the Maratha Chiefs in Western India). But until some such appropriation was made, the 'Waste' was used by the people who happened to reside in the neighbourhood. Probably if there were some specially valuable trees like *teak* or *sandal-wood,* they would be called 'royal trees,' and none would be cut without permisson or without payment of a fee. In the old Hindu States of Oudh, I find mention of the Rajas levying an 'axe-tax' (tangarahi) in the forest. No one then thought of defining or asking whether the villages had a 'right' to graze, and whether such 'rights' were 'in gross' or were 'appendant' to the tenement or estate. At best there was an indefinite sort of understanding, that certain localities should be left as 'jungle' for grazing and wood-cutting. In modern times, when it became necessary to provide for such useful and long-established practices on a legal basis, it was thought best to deal with them as if they had been regular prescriptive rights, and not try and draw any fine distinctions. But in so doing the law provides (and with more than usual reason) that the 'rights' thus liberally conceded, are to be restricted to what is just and proper on principles of general law. No right, for example, to burn the forest or do any *destructive* act, is recognized in any case; and also rights are not allowed to remain unlimited or indefinite; they are to be recorded within definite limits, and confined to the person (or estate) as well as to the purpose, for which they were intended (p. 291), and they are to be exercised subject to fair regulation." He further adds, "It is extraordinary what loose and inaccurate ideas on this subject sometimes prevail. Supposing that (in India) a forest is situated where there are several village-groups in the vicinity, and that a very considerable number of villagers have

> been in the long-continued habit (1) of cutting trees for their house-holding, (2) of grazing cattle, (3) of cutting brush and small-wood for fuel, (4) of raking up the dead, decaying leaves and humus for manure, (5) of collecting leaves or lopping twigs for fodder, (6) of gathering herbage, moss and grass, for litter. People sometimes talk as if, at any rate, the *collective amount of these rights* made the people owners of the forest. This is entirely a mistake; the ownership of the forest still remains in the State or in the landlord, or whoever it is that, under the circumstances of the case, and in the progress of time, is or has become, the owner." (Baden-Powell, "Forest Law," pages 282-283, 285.)

The extent to which easements to forest produce have had to be recognized is easily understood from a reading of the following list given by Mr. Baden-Powell.

"List of Forest-Produce Easements"

A. Rights to wood.	1. For building.	
	2. For industry and agricultural implements.	
	3. For fuel.	Brushwood. Billet-wood. Dead-wood. Torches.
	4. For conversion, or production of some substance.	*Cutch*-boiling. Tarmaking (and wood oil). Charcoal. Lime-kilns.
B. Rights of pasture of grazing.		
C. Rights of grass-cutting (including all herbage, but not branches of trees).		
D. Rights of litter (dead leaves and twigs, moss, etc.; scraping up the humus).		

E. Rights of lopping trees (whether for fodder or litter).

Rosin, natural varnish, wood-oil rubber, etc.

Roots.

F. Rights to collect minor produce

Drugs, plants, flowers and leaves.
Fruits and seeds.
Bark and fibres,
Clay, sand, gravel, limestone, pebbles, concrete, etc.

G. Hunting and fishing.

H. Practice (not properly a right) of shifting cultivation."

(Page 319, Baden-Powell, Ibid)

> The rights of villagers in general "can never (from its nature) be co-extensive with the ownership, and can, therefore, never extend to swallowing up the whole; for that would be, in fact, attacking the substance of the estate itself, and rendering it practically useless to the owner. As no easement (of produce) can be *unlimited*, it may be said that the question of extent or quantity—how much material, what number of cattle, and so forth—is involved in the nature of the easement. This depends on the terms of the grant or other title; and in the large class of cases where the right is prescriptive, *i.e.*, has long existed openly and peaceably, but without any (traceable) original grant, the law makes express provision for determining these matters, usually on the basis of the actual needs or requirements of the right-holder." (Baden-Powell, Ibid pp. 79-86.)

The effects of legal definition as applied to rights in waste-land, are recognized by Dr. Sanderson.

> "The common-lands were the *real estate* of the village community. When these lands were enclosed by the political control of the manor-owners or were divided by permission of the state, the small tenants and cottagers were left without means of subsistence other than wages, and the foundation of the village structure was destroyed." (Sanderson, Ibid, page 420.)

In conclusion it is well to recognize the viewpoint stated by Mr. Kung Chuan Hsiao. He points out that:

> "although solidarity is an essential requisite in social organization, it does not exhaust the entire meaning of social organization,

which, on account of its variable content, cannot be placed upon the same level with the symbiotical phenomena of certain plant organisms. Human society is a far more complex matter than these. At certain stages of men's social life, it is true, solidarity seems to be sole consideration; the beginning of any community, as Aristotle long ago said, is marked by the need for mutual help and assistance, without which men would perish in a struggle with the unfriendly forces of nature. This fact of solidarity, indeed, is observable even in societies of quite advanced character when they are confronted with imminent crises or external dangers. At other times, however, solidarity seems to be of comparatively less importance. For as men are endowed with the 'sense of good and evil', the ethical and ideal elements in their thinking constantly tend to free them from the seemingly unalterable determinism of social laws. History affords a wealth of instances of men who, influenced by abstract ethical principles, have been willing to sacrifice life, comfort, and even the existing social peace itself in order to attain something which they regarded more desirable than a mere system of perfectly adjusted co-operative living. The principle of solidarity, therefore, seems to be a wholly inadequate principle of social organization; if it simply asserts the elementary interdependence of men in their basic needs, it is almost a truism, which writers from Aristotle down unanimously admit; if it is intended to serve as an ultimate criterion of all social life, it leaves our higher and more important social experiences out of account." (K. C. Hsiao, "Political Pluralism", pages 226-227.)

3. The Jajmani System in relation to the functional group.

(*a*) *Advantages*

The group system of organization found in the Hindu Jajmani system, is adequate in that it recognizes that "any given society, is composed, not of an aggregate of individuals, but of an assemblage of groups." Professor Catlin continues:

"Although there has been, among many political theorists and statesmen, a singular reluctance to admit the legitimate function played in social life by parties, the abolition of all groups could only happen if the spirit of friendship, which draws together men similar and of like outlook and interests, and the spirit of hatred of that which we consider evil and injurious, were eradicated. Groups are a natural expression of the diversities and likenesses existing in the human mind and are individual character writ large. Clashes between groups can only be overcome and their interests and divergent outlooks harmonized in terms of a broader and dominant loyalty. Where this greater loyalty is not equally and generally shared, peace in a society is only maintained by the domination of one group, with its interests, outlook, ideals, and the conventions convenient to it, over the others." (George E. G. Catlin, "A Study of the Principles of Politics", Page 268-769.)

According to the caste system each group has its particular function in society as shown in Section I, so that there is no confusion in function. The village community is prepared to accept in its organization any caste that performs a necessary function. Where the demand is slight no encouragement is given to the caste to settle. Representatives of two such castes, the *Tamboli* (seller of the betel leaf) and the *Ahir* (cattle raiser) formerly lived in the village. When they left, no effort was made by the village to invite others of their caste to take their place. They were not essential to the village economy.

Professor Ross emphasizes the influence of prestige in a community. Although the high caste men are given special prestige according to religious ideas held by the Hindus, yet each caste has its own prestige in reference to its own peculiar function. A potter, a carpenter, an iron worker and a goldsmith, have a prestige through their own able performance of function which is peculiar to themselves. Before they looked to outside markets they produced beautiful articles. The distribution of these functions through castes creates a balance in the community which makes for co-operation, satisfaction and peace. Another balancing power is described by Professor Catlin as being that of wealth and power. He states that "wealth and power should be divided, as has largely been the case in the past in the clerical and learned professions." (Catlin Ibid, Page 363.) This is achieved by the Hindu system in that it encourages the Brahmans who are the highest in the social scale to seek spiritual power rather than wealth. The result of balanced functioning such as we find in the different castes, is social solidarity.

(*b*) *Disadvantages*

But the group system of organization in the Hindu Jajmani System is inadequate in that it makes these groups hereditary. Mukerjee points out in defence of the Hindu system, that

> "Social stratification becomes the result of a gradual upward economic differentiation, and the social hierarchy in the main corresponds to the steps of economic advance, the forester and the shepherd standing lowest, the artisans and peasants in the middle, the traders and landlords, tribal chiefs and priests at the top of the socio-economic scale. All this reproduces in the life of a single community the whole course of cultural development." (Mukerjee, Ibid Page 268.)

This would be true if the "steps of advance" had not ceased. The instant caste groupings were fixed by birth and interlocked by marriage within the same caste group only, the cultural development made possible by this system, ceased. The Hindus in establishing an equilibrium in society, failed to recognize that the groups within its jurisdiction were human and hence variable. This variableness of human groups requires a constant re-establishment of equilibrium and a freedom to make that adjustment—perhaps on the same or perhaps on a different level—and the failure to recognize this nature of groups constitutes a major weakness in the Hindu Jajmani System.

In accommodating Mohammedan groups in the system, it may appear that the Hindu Jajmani System is capable of adapting itself to change in religious belief on the part of some of its groups. This is only in part true because the Mohammedan groups are discouraged from publicly celebrating Mohammedan religious festivals and encouraged to partake in Hindu religious festivals. One Mohammedan in the village went so far in order to ingratiate his Brahman jajman, as to permit his son to wear a "chutiya" (Hindu scalp lock.) This could not possibly be tolerated by a faithful follower of Mohammed.

A further weakness of the Hindu Jajmani System has to do with the position of the lowest functional groups, or lowest castes. The higher castes although they cannot move up in the scale of occupations, can move down, and the higher the caste, the greater the choice of occupations. But those who are the lowest have nothing left to which to descend and they cannot ascend. They are shut up to nothing but the dregs of occupatoinal tasks. Even a greater weakness is the attitude of the higher castes to the low. Quotations from Manu given in the earlier part of this study reveal that the Sudra has the relationship of a slave to the Brahman. This relationship holds particularly for the lowest Hindu groups, such as the leather workers and sweepers in Karimpur. In actual practice we find that the position is not exactly that of a slave because of the freedom of movement given to these groups, but in social attitudes it is little better than that of a relationship between a master and slave. A comparison between the position held by some "kam-karnewalas" in

Karimpur and the position of the predial and agrestic slaves described in William Adam's "The Law and Custom of Slavery in British India" published in 1840 enable one to see how minor are the differences. Payments in kind are similar, work required is the same. The only difference is in the nature of the bonds. In slavery the master has a title deed to his slave. In the jajmani system the jajman has a title deed to everything that is dear to a "kam-karne-wala", namely his livelihood and that of his family. "A Sudra, though emancipated by his master, is not released from a state of servitude; for a state which is natural to him, by whom can he be divested." ("A Digest of Hindu Law on Contracts and Successions" with a commentary by Jagannatha Tercapanchanana by H. T. Colebrooke, 1801. Pages 232, 233, Vol. II.)

As a contrast to the servile position of the low castes we have the lordly position of the Brahman. That the jajmani system has worked so well is a credit to large hosts of Brahmans who have understood their duty to be not merely that of self-development but the care of others in their own community, who were dependent on them. The weakness of the system shows in those spots where the Brahmans have used their position for power rather than for service. Where they have desired to add wealth to their power they have violated a fundamental principle of the jajmani system, that balance was best maintained by separating wealth and power. In the form that society takes outside of the village community, wealth is the valued commodity and as more and more Brahmans make contact with the outside world the greater will be the temptation and the greater the number who are unwilling to meet the ideals set before them by their early teachings. Hence, the weakness is leaving the destinies of the low castes in the hands of the high.

The cash value of the system to the individual group is not great enough to attract qualified professional services such as that of medical men, legal advisers, spiritual advisors, educators, etc. It does not provide adequately for large families, for example the case of the oil-pressers and seamsters in Karimpur. The father in each case had sufficient for himself, but there was not enough to meet the needs of three sons and their families. With a lack of effort on the part of some of the jajmans to meet standardized rates, there is created a feeling of insecurity on the part of the "kam karnewalas". With the decline of the power of the *Panchayat* the misdemeanors of the jajmans go by, unchallenged, and the faith of the "kam-karnewalas" in the system is weakened.

4. The Jajmani System in relation to the individual.

(*a*) *Advantages*

The individualist may feel that this system can in no way be adequate for the individual. But the parties to the Hindu Jajmani System cannot be considered to be bound.

> "If the master has the right to recapture the servant who leaves his service, or even if he has the right to call upon the officers of the state to pursue him and bring him back, to his work, then we may account this servant as unfree man, albeit the relation between him and his master has been created by free contract." (F. W. Maitland, "Domesday Book and Beyond", Page 42.)

The "kam-karnewala" himself does not have to perform the service.

> "A grant to a man and his heirs on condition of performing service, does not in general mean that the service is to be per-

sonally performed by the grantee or his heirs, but that the grantee is to be responsible for its performance." (Herbert Cowell, "The Indian Digest", page 762.)

The Hindu Jajmani System must, therefore, be considered as *etats libres*.

"Although possessed of police power they are, owing to ease of access and egress, *etats libres* (in Russeau's sense of the world) such as it is neither legally nor economically impossible for the individual or family to quit, and are in effect voluntary societies. As voluntary, they are entitled to draw the logical conclusions of their own accepted principles and to enforce a single moral system upon those who choose to be members of them. The conventions which obtain in such communities can rise to far more exacting heights than those of a State, because their law is not the highest common factor of a compulsorily gathered and heterogeneous aggregate. In such voluntary communities the tension and friction between involuntary minorities and dominant majorities can be reduced to a minimum. Towards such communities, be it a nation or be it some like-minded group of more exacting and detailed standards, the religious spirit of man, which seeks a cessation of the strife of ambition and of the chaffering about interests, naturally turns. The like-minded community can alone at once satisfy, by its co-operation in procuring for each appropriate gratifications, and allay, by its atmosphere of mutual understanding and guarantee, the pursuit of power, whose parents are the undying emotions of hope and of fear. Here alone is the, solution of the fundamental antinomies of Politics." (Catlin Ibid, p. 422-423.)

The freedom of the individual within the Hindu Jajmani System is somewhat restricted but it is not without its definite advantages. "The will is the servant of the wish, and a wish which moves easily within the prison of convention knows no restriction in obedience to law. The law has only terrors for the law-breaker, custom is only obnoxious to the innovator, subordination to the man of ambitions, and control for him who is irked by it when new wishes seize him. But when restraint has become conscious constraint, already a wish has been formed for that which is beyond the limits, which wish is now reinforced by the constraint-hating will. Hence education may be a great disruptive influence, by enlarging men's wishes, or a great conservative force, by conventionalizing them."

"The secret, therefore of procuring a happier adjustment than by constraint, without very elaborate or troublesome changes of the balance, is to represent convention as a restraint arising from the unalterable nature of things, and by habituating the minds of the members of a community to a limited and well-known circle of wishes and demands, moral, religious, political, or whatever it may be. This circle comes to constitute an unquestioned ideal of what ought to be wished, and so long as the mass of the community can be brought to concur with this ideal, there is no need to readjust conventions which have been constructed in accordance with this generally held and stabilized ideal, or which, as the mores of the time and place, are its parents......This common good, which all are induced to wish for, will be regarded by all as reasonable, since all, wishing the same, find their wills parallel and hence the social system harmonious, non-contradictory, and reasonable. The harmony appears to rest, when the tune is set by those who accept a common ideal, upon something less discordant than the stress of forces and tugging of wills." (Catlin, Ibid, pages 285-287.)

It is a system which provides for the individual, the stability of social order, rather than mere social existence, as differentiated by Catlin.

"What harmony of wills exists at any time is due to an exercise of intelligence, which discovers a method, and of energy, which maintains men in an order in which the activities of each are generally consistent with the activities of the other. Everyone contributes to this energy necessary for the maintenance of stability in so far as, spontaneous co-operation apart, he deliberately exercises himself to support authority. This harmony, which it requires energy to attain and maintain, does not arise from some extraneous uniting force, such as the divine will of God considered as transcendent or the command of a semidivine legislator or a sovereign prince considered as in a state of nature over against society, but from the wills of the members of society.

Energy which might have been expended in conflict is, so far as a guarantee is concerned of our present powers and rights, more economically expended in maintaining authority. *Social order*, in brief, as distinct from *social existence* in the sense of mutual interdependence and of contiguity in family life—in the sense, that is, of inability to avoid our neighbours or to avoid influencing or being influenced by them, is not a natural fact. Solidarity is more than mutuality. Fundamentally, social order is the product of a balance of wills in a condition of energy." (Catlin, Ibid, pages 195-197.)

Mr. Colebrooke writes:

"Indeed, throughout India, the relation of master and slave appears to impose the duty of protection and cherishment on the master as much as that of fidelity and obedience on the slave, and their mutual conduct is consistent with the sense of such an obligation; since it is marked with gentleness and indulgence on the one side, and with zeal and loyalty on the other." (Colebrooke, H. T., "Remarks on the Husbandry and Internal Commerce of Bengal", page 129.)

"The protection of life and the protection of the good life alike must involve the maintenance of a peaceful order, as a condition, if man is to live either securely or well......Social organization has been successfully built up through the ages as a bulwark against strife, and is firmly based upon the co-operative interlocking of wills. Whereas in the biological struggle overt conflict is more patent than co-ordination, in the political conflict the converse is true and the peaceful community is more in evidence than warring bodies......In the political society of any civilization other than the most savage, the absolute hostility of individual against individual has been transformed or replaced by a more effective form of defence and offence, the alliance of individuals in groups against other groups. The potential hostility of individual to individual is allayed by the recognition of methods of co-ordinating wills, for defence, offence, and common purposes, under social conventions and laws. The requirements of success in the maintenance of interests compel this intelligent co-operation in a social system which is preexistent to the particular individual and his wishes......The human will is not free, but is dependent for the content of its willing upon the stimulus of the whole complex of the interdependent environments, and for the intensity of its determination upon the intensity of that stimulus in immediate experience or in memory......'This association founded on community of interest', continues Ratzenhofer, 'is no arbitrary act of individuals but an individual and social necessity'." (Catlin, Ibid, p. 187, p. 191-194.)

This system enables custom to make its greatest contribution. Dr. Ross says:

"There must be some recognized authority to draw the line of demarcation between conflicting interests. In a static society, custom can run such a line. But when there is change and progress, such lines become uncertain; and if there is no external authority to draw them afresh, society dissolves in chaos. The system for the control of conduct, while it stimulates *sympathy sociability*, and the sense of *equity*, greatly narrows the sphere of *resentment*." (Ross, "Social Control", page 40.)

As observers of this system from October 1925 to March 1931, we can testify to the general contentment of the people of Karimpur. Dr. Catlin says:

"The test of social health is actual contentment or at least a vigorous constitution capable of remaining unaffected by local disorders. Educational sedatives, from the Platonic to the Fascist or Marxian myths, may be applied, so long as they in fact effect a cure instead of being merely narcotics or palliatives. The preaching of a doctrine of social obligation will healthfully encourage the enjoyment of duty, will produce in those who accept it the psychological satisfaction of feeling at one with the community, and will cure those neurotic diseases of dissatisfaction which may arise more from an irritant ideology than from any detectable maladjustments between men or groups. But to speak of 'inculcating a respect for Authority' (in general) is as meaningless as to speak of 'inculcating a respect for production' (in general). The question is whether the authority contributes to the good of the individual and of all his, as he understands this good, or at least facilitates his and their attainment of that good as far as is possible under the social circumstances." (Catlin, Ibid, pages 452-3.)

Finally, let us hear an Indian in defence of the Hindu system.

"Law, according to the Hindu theory, sets the end and limit for the State, and the State is only the enforcing agent for the end set by the social purpose shared in by all individuals and groups. This reads as sentences from Duguit's *L'Etat.* Duguit is largely influenced by the solidarity doctrine of Durkheim, according to whom men form by nature a unitary group in which the interests of the individual are bound up with those of his fellows. That individuality grows with sociality is the most precious of Eastern experiences, and it has found institutional expression throughout the East, being incorporated into her characteristic types of communalistic law and polity. Communalism encourages the unanimity of minds and wills of groups and would develop norms of social co-operaton which protect society against absolutism in the State on the one hand, and the clash of group interests on the other. This is possible because communalism in the East represents as we have seen, a principle of social grouping in which the including group stands not for partial, hypostasised interests of the segmented man, but for the concrete interest and representing the whole personality. On the other hand, the greatest difficulty of Western reformers has been both an increasing number of group loyalties, which actually and actively compete for mastery, and the absence of vitality in the local group organization on which they have to depend ultimately for counteracting the rigidity of the party system and for creating a united will, a genuine public opinion. In the East the daily lives of the people are within the area of government through the myriad local bodies and village communities which exercise the restraining force of custom, and are a unification of group interests, and public opinion, in the realization of a true community life. These are the original and essential foundations of Eastern polity, of an active, responsible and creative sociality. This alone can lift politics from a mere wrangle of opposing interests. The East has developed a good deal of organic or functional solidarity based upon social specialization and division of labour. This furnishes the necessary guidance for the individual and the basis of social and political control. But, unlike the West, the occupational group does not here comprehend the majority of the interests of individuals. Extra-economic interests and values here have received a recognition in social structure denied to Western society that since the Industrial Revolution has come to be primarily industrial in its foundations. The family, the clan and the village gentry in China, the caste, the guild and the village community in India, are left by the State to settle their own problems. Within each function, again, there is some degree of representation and delegation. But, on the other hand, no effort has been made in recent reconstruction to relate this socio-economic federalism to the categories of the political structure. In the social history of the East, the occupational group is placed in the harmonious setting of the village community which comprehends the diverse needs of specialized functional or professional groups and ministers to the varied needs of human life." (Mukerjee, "Democracies of the East", pages 351-353.)

(*b*) *Disadvantages*

Individual freedom and aspiration is decidedly affected by this system. There is very little stimulus for better work. The washerman has no desire to buy a flat iron to iron his jajman's clothes. If he were to get one he would simply increase his own labour and get very little if any more, pay for it. The leather worker does not make shoes. The added labour would be out of proportion to his added pay. Self-assertion is discouraged. There are two bangle-sellers in Karimpur, one a docile old man, the other an assertive young man. The jajmans all stand by the old man because he is so "simple". The young man on the other hand has to go elsewhere for his jajmans because he is a "troublesome fellow". Self-assertion is not a desideratum for a "kam karnewala".

There is no individuality in the sense understood by a Westerner.

"Men are regarded and treated, not as individuals, but always as members of a particular group. Everybody is first a citizen, and then, as a citizen, he is a member of his order—of an aristocracy or a democracy, of an order of patricians or plebians; or in those societies which an unhappy fate has afflicted with a special perversion in their course of development, of a caste. Next, he is a member of a gens, house or clan; and lastly, he is a member of his family. This last was the narrowest and most personal relation in which he stood; nor, paradoxical as it may seem, was he ever regarded as himself, as a distinct individual. His individuality was swallowed up in his family. I repeat the definition of a primitive society given before. It has for its units not individuals, but groups of men united by the reality or the fiction of blood-relationship". (H. S. Maine, "Ancient Law", pages 177-178.)

The individual who profits most from the system is the Brahman. Sir Henry Sumner Maine writes,

> "I have myself heard an Indian Brahman dispute it (theory of Equality) on the ground that, according to the clear teaching of his religion, a Brahman was entitled to twenty times as much happiness as anybody else." (Maine, "The Early History of Institutions", Page 399.)

The one who profits least is the low caste menial.

> "The powers possessed by masters or owners over their slaves are absolute. Hindu law 'treats the slave as the property of his master, familiarly speaking of this species of property in association with cattle, under the contemptuous designation of bipeds and quadrupeds. It makes no provision for the protection of the slave from the cruelty and ill-treatment of an unfeeling master, nor defines the master's power over the person of his slave; neither prescribing distinct limits to that power, nor declaring it to extend to life or limb. It allows to the slave no right of property even in his own acquisitions, except by the indulgence of his master'." (Wm. Adam. "The Law and Custom of Slavery in British India", Page 17.)

With this kind of behaviour there can be no equality. Equality was not the aim of those who devised the Hindu Jajmani System.

> "If Aryans and non-Aryans inter-change their occupations and conduct (the one taking that of the other, there is) equality (between them)." (Buhler, "The Sacred Laws of the Aryas" Page 231. Vol. II, Sacred Books of the East.)

And finally this system gives rise to what psychologists recognize as "slave-mentality", a mentality that is reflected in the "*hath jhorke*" method of approach, (described on Page 97) and the deferential attitude shown by servile castes in the presence of their more favoured jajmans. It leads to a fatalistic conception of life which feeds on superstition and is easily influenced by those who are unscrupulous enough to exploit their ignorance. These attitudes through the course of years have crystallized into customs which have given a "certain contentedness and satisfaction, but at the price of an inhibition of progress." (Sanderson, "The Rural Community," Page 404.)

> "In societies of an archaic type, a particular craft or kind of knowledge becomes in time an hereditary profession of families, almost as a matter of course. The difficulty with a native of India, unsophisticated by English ideas, is not to find a reason why a son should succeed to the learning of his father, and consequently to his office and duties; his difficulty would rather be to explain to himself why it should not be so, and how the public interests could be consulted by any other arrangement." (Maine, "The Early History of Institutions", Page 245..)

Conclusion

Having observed the structure of the Hindu Jajmani System, the functions, compensations and rights of its component parts, disintegrating factors at work within the system, and the adequacies and inadequacies of the system, we are in a position to attempt an analysis of the value of the Hindu Jajmani System as a service inter-relationship system in a rural community today.

The village community like any other natural group consists of human relationships. The smaller the community, the more intimate and closely interrelated those relationships may become. Where the members of the community are a unity in that they are bound together by a common ancestry, common worship, common totem, common property, or common function, they work for common aims, and the individual gains his highest expression in working for the community group. Just as the family is strong in so far as the members subordinate themselves to the larger group, so is the community strong in so far as the individuals or groups in a community subordinate themselves to the larger group. The Hindu Jajmani System represents an interrelationship built up on clearly defined function. It represents the organization of a community based on the Hindu belief that God "assigned separate duties and occupations to each individual from birth," these duties being as fixed as the functions of a father and mother in a family. Its strength in giving stability and psychical integration to Indian village communities through centuries is undisputed. It is demonstrated in what exists today in Karimpur and by the observations of numerous authorities quoted in this study. It possesses many features which are the envy of modern rural communities today.

It is built up on the assumption that functional abilities are fixed and transmitted from generation to generation, that exchange of services must be on an asymmetrical level, and that ethical and ideal elements in the thinking of the individuals remain constant. If these assumptions were psychologically correct, the world would find in the Hindu Jajmani System a system that would be worthy of adoption in every community. But the assumptions are not correct, and the system as now constituted cannot continue with the introduction of intellectual freedom. Leather workers and sweepers once convinced of intellectual ability are no longer content to perform the menial tasks, sweep the roads and clean the privies. And Brahmans who prove themselves intellectually inferior cannot lay claim to the right to teach those who are his intellectual superiors, even though of more humble birth.

Illustrations of such instances are readily found in India. A leather worker who built up for himself a reputation as a builder, furnished an office in his village home. His traditional high caste jajmans objected. They informed him that if there were to be any offices, they would be in their homes and not in the house of a leather worker. The leather worker in order to maintain the dignity of his new profession needed an office. Since he could not have it in the village, he moved away. His jajmans succeeded in blocking some of his efforts to buy property, but not all of them. The leather worker then built several houses for himself and his friends in a nearby city and is continuing uninterrupted in his material development. Boys of sweeper families, who have become Christians, have been sent away to Mission schools and colleges for their education. Some of them have become college professors, doctors, etc. They return to their old village home for a visit, and their jajmans would give them brooms and tell them to get back to their traditional work if they could control their actions. However, the failure of the system to provide intellectual freedom to its members should not blind us to its definite value of service inter-relationship.

In an analysis of the system, we ask: A. What can we learn from this system? B. What is there in the system that should be protected and continued? And C. What is there in the system that is of value to the West?

What can we learn from this system?

1. Contentment and peace are attainable goals for a rural community.

We may here repeat Catlin's words, which well describe the situation as we find it in Karimpur.

> "The preaching of a doctrine of social obligation will healthfully encourage the enjoyment of duty, will produce in those

> who accept it the psychological satisfaction of feeling at one with the community, and will cure those neurotic diseases of dissatisfaction which may arise more from an irritant ideology than from any detectable maladjustments between men or groups. (Catlin, Study of the Principles of Politics, pages 452-453.)

2. In a contented and peaceful community, the individual must subordinate his wishes to those of a group.

We find in Karimpur that the individuals are ready to co-operate for the common good. Havell claims that the Hindus

> "took their allotted shares of work for the common weal..... by a clear perception of mutual advantage and a voluntary recognition of superior intellectual leadership." (The History of Aryan Rule in India, pages 9-13.)

This may be rationalization, but it has its values as shown on pages 170 and 171.

3. A federation of groups in a community leads to real social solidarity.

We find in Karimpur, 24 distinct functional groups which find their strength in federated inter-activity. Catlin says, "Groups are a natural expression of the diversities and likenesses existing in the human mind and are individual character writ large. Clashes between groups can only be overcome and their interests and divergent outlooks harmonized in terms of a broader and dominant loyalty." (Ibid, 268-269.) Although we may not feel that the groups existing in Karimpur represent the "natural expression of the diversities and likenesses" of the residents of Karimpur, yet the principal stands.

4. A federation of groups in a community needs a central authority. This is supplied by the Panchayat.

The Panchayat with its method of adjusting differences; its respect for common standards of wishes and demands, be they moral, religious, economic, or political, which make up the mores and the social heritage of the community; and its recognition of the spirit of mutual aid, equity and obligation for the common welfare, makes possible "protection and all that law and custom, conventions and institutions, can give to thc individual of assurance by stabilizing control." (Catlin, Ibid, 96.)

The court records seem to show that the Brahmans through appeals to the Higher Courts are continually strengthening their jajmani rights. The lower caste groups on the other hand, because of the lack of finance, the weakness of the Panchayat, or absence of friends to represent their cause, are steadily allowing their rights to disintegrate. The ill-effects of having a mere shell of authority in the existing Panchayat in Karimpur has been described on pages 124 and 140. Instances similar to those stated will multiply as the forces of disintegration gain in impetus.

5. Those engaged in agriculture may enjoy the advantages of real community life, by living in the village rather than on their farms.

Sanderson points out, as quoted on page 156, that the art of agriculture has been perfected under the protection of the village community. The vocation of agriculture still continues and it serves as a basis for a strong common interest. Physical environment "defines the areas of association....The desire of peoplc for sociability, for recognition and response, forms a bond of the rural community." (Ibid, pages 664, 665.) This is undoubtedly the viewpoint of the rcsidents of Karimpur.

6. The village community has been and is at present the primary political, social, economic and religious unit of society in India, and its sutonomy should be recognized in any future reorganization.

Mukerjee urges throughout his books that the best system of national government would be that which would recognize the village community as the natural unit of federal organization. He states,

> "The most difficult thing for a foreigner to understand about the village community is that it is a functional and territorial group in one, representing and fulfilling common interests, economic, juridical and religious......Instead of developing towards a centralized and bureaucratic parliamentarism it is necessary here to give state recognition to the village-communities and to those occupational, communal and functional units which show a large measure of popular government internally, and to provide the méans for unorganized units to pass into the stage of organization and recognition in a federal and representative system." (Mukerjee, Democracies of the East, pages 354, 355.)

This advice should apply not only to the foreigner but to the Indian landlord and Indian administrator as well.

7. Education plays a large part in creating unity of community purpose.

Through a period extending over 1,500 or more years the people of India have been taught the tenants of Brahmanism with its functional division of occupations. Gradually all came to recognize that the "common good which all (were) induced to wish for (was) regarded by all as reasonable, since all, wishing the same, (found) their wills parallel and hence the social system harmonious, non-contradictory and reasonable." (Catlin, Ibid page 287.) In this manner all members of a community are led to have a common interest.

8. A satisfactory and balanced relationship between server and served, no matter whom the individuals, must be developed on a symmetrical level.

Colebrook points out that the master-slave relationship in India is that of "protection and cherishment" on the part of the master, and "fidelity and obedience" on the part of the slave. And again, "gentleness and indulgence" on the part of the master, and "zeal and loyalty" on the part of the slave. (Colebrook, H. T., Remarks on the Husbandry and Internal Commerce of Bengal, page 129.) This very excellently describes the relationship between high caste jajmans and low caste "kam karnewalas" but does not describe the relationship between low caste jajmans and high caste "kam karnewalas". We find here an asymmetrical relationship of service. The "slave-mentality" attitude predominates in the low caste man whether he is serving or being served. Just as each occupational group has been given the prestige of being the one and only group performing a given function and is therefore worthy of protection and cherishment, so should each in turn as they commend the services of others be they high born or low born, be entitled to fidelity, obedience, zeal and loyalty. The relationship between server and served must be symmetrical in all group relationships. Each must take his turn at being lord and each his turn as servant.

9. Asymmetrical relationships as between groups in community must be by common consent, subject to change and not fixed.

No community is without asymmetrical relationships as between individuals or between groups. Deference is shown to different types of individuals or groups, dependent on the type of society living in the community. The deference shown to Brahmans in Karimpur is not, in many cases, due to a recognition of value or merit but due to a recognition of the autocracy of birth. In some cases Brahmans would by common consent be given this deference as real community leaders. This is as it should be. The weakness of the Hindu Jajmani System is not that it has in it asymmetrical relationships, but that these relationships are fixed. Its weakness is that common consent is "frozen". No opportunity has been given to the members of the groups within the last 2,000 years, to express an opinion that might alter the relationships in the community. Common consent may have been taken when the caste system was first organized; but it has not been taken since.

10. There must be flexibility enough in a village group organization to accommodate variations due to changing conditions, internal and external.

The section describing disintegrating factors at work in the Hindu Jajmani System reveals its inability to make adjustments to changing conditions. Forces (See Sanderson, pages 653, 654) far more subtle than those of the armed forces that sought to take away wives, daughters and property, are now at work, and adjustments have to be made to them, otherwise the system must collapse. Sanderson states:

> "The problem of the community group is one of both internal and external adaptation; to adjust itself to the existing environment and to readjust itself to the ever-new environment, but also to re-create the environment to meet its unsatisfied desires, through communication, discovery and invention, through science, art, and religion. The process is ever one of adjusting the old culture, institutions, and social attitudes to new attitudes necessitated by new values arising from the changed environment, and of creating new attitudes which will provide a more satisfying social relationship; this adjustment is a process not only of adaptation but of creation, so that it is ever recurring and never completed." (Sanderson, Ibid, pages 646-647.)

11. Economic isolation leads to a low standard of living.

No one who is accustomed to a western standard of living can enthuse over a standard of living which, although seemingly adequate for subsistence, is as meagre as that offered to the average "kam karnewala" in Karimpur. Only ten of the families in Karimpur in 1926 could find through the performance of the occupational function alone a living adequate to meet even this low standard of subsistense. They included 1 Nai, 1 Brahman, 2 Sunars, 4 Darzis, 1 Dhobi and 1 Faqir. Practically all have to supplement their earnings by tilling a bit of soil. The risks of poverty are too great for an adequate enjoyment of life, and permanently prevent any desires for the amenities of life.

12. An economic system built around waste lands cannot be permanent.

Mr. Baden-Powell's excellent presentation of this subject, reference to which is made in the previous section, makes it clear that a village system built so largely on the easements of waste land cannot permanently stand. A landlord of my acquaintance after being advised by a government agricultural specialist, set about ploughing up some of his waste land. He met with a storm of protest from his tenants to the effect that in so doing he would be robbing the village cattle or of their grazing facilities, which in turn would very materially affect their livelihood. As he was personally not in special need of the extra income that could be realized from this waste land, he gave way to their protests and the ploughing was stopped. Such conditions cannot go on forever. The agricultural experts in India are educating landlords to the possibilities of their waste lands and in time these must go. With their going will go the many privileges which are now enjoyed by villagers, such as those in Karimpur. Pressure for the use of the waste lands of Karimpur has not as yet been felt, since the two landlords who at present own the village, own large estates and live 40 and 110 miles away.

13. One must have a genuine respect for the builders of the Hindu caste system and its co-ordinating patterns.

Authorities are at variance as to whether the caste system was organized by the Dravadians, the original inhabitants of India or by the Aryan invaders. We cannot therefore locate the real initiators of the system. But the intricacies of the system as worked out practically in every day life and as described in this study cannot but command the admiration of every student of rural social organization. Its persistence in its general structure throughout centuries is adequate support of the contention that they not only built thoroughly but well. In form it is woven in as intricate a pattern as some of the hand-woven cloth that has won the admiration of other nations since the beginning of their commerce with India.

14. Religion is a powerful social force for unifying interest and for furnishing the incentive to build a strong community life.

The Hindu Jajmani System has as its central core the belief that God himself intended that society should be organized as is described in these pages. As has already been indicated, the various functions to be performed by the different castes are a biological fact representing inherent differences in physical and mental traits irrevocable except through the intervention of God himself.* "C. Bougle, in his study of the India caste regime, has come to the conclusion that without the religious factor neither the origin nor the long existence of the caste system

*See Page 99 ffg.

are comprehensible." (Sorokin, Contemporary Sociological Theories, Page 669.) The place held by religion as a social control of man's conduct is brought out by numerous writers. But more convincing still is the system that we have been studying in these pages. The threads of religion are woven through and through, and very few changes can be made without breaking one or more of those threads.

15. The greatest contributing factor to a sense of security and social insurance in a village community is the recognition of its common responsibility for the livelihood of all its members, including its own dependents, delinquents and defectives.

The strength of the Hindu Jajmani System is its all-inclusiveness. No accustomed want can arise for which provision is not made—land, food, seed, clothing, legal help, religious counsel, and numerous other types of help enumerated in this study. Various attempts have been made in India by reformers. to build model villages on an individualistic basis. Most of them have failed because they are unable to give their members the security offered by a village enjoying jajmani relationships. A pattern of this type is not acquired in a day. It is the work of centuries. Numerous co-operative societies have attempted to replace jajmans by introducing a rigid credit system. Where wise managers have given the credit a flexibility like that offered by a jajman they have survived. Otherwise they have failed. Those who would do away with unscrupulous jajmans must themselves be prepared to establish a jajmani relationship, and accept all the obligations that are listed in Section II.

Villagers are loathe to give up their jajmani compensations and rights. Occasionally one of them ventures to go to the city where he receives money wages more than equivalent to his income from the jajmani system. He takes the cash, but feels injured when he finds that he is no longer entitled to the old perquisites. Furthermore, he is not able to spend so much money wisely. When his wages stop, there is no place for him to fit in. There are no more tragic figures in India than the unemployed who have no village home. This love for the security of the village is the despair of mill and factory owners, because very few labourers are willing to settle permanently in a factory area. The security of the village community is its strength.

We could easily lose ourselves in a discussion of the degree of freedom necessary for each individual and become involved in a lengthy discussion as to the relative merits of the philosophical theories of freedom *vs.* solidarity, absolute egotism *vs.* unlimited altruism, individualistic-liberal *vs.* communalistic-conservative societies, equality *vs.* inequality, static *vs.* dynamic societies, economic determinism *vs.* social organization and control, economic subsistence *vs.* economic anarchy, and socilaism *vs.* capitalism. Facts of value in the presentation of all of these theories are found in this analysis of the Hindu Jajmani System, but they must be reserved for further studies. Personally, the writer agrees with the statement that "an individualistic theory of politics, in the real sense, is a contradiction of terms." (Kung Chuan Hsiao, Political Pluralism, Pages 240, 241.)

What is there in the system that should be protected and continued?

1. Its general contentment and peace should be retained.

It may be paradoxical to think that the Hindu Jajmani System cannot continue as it now exists, yet that the general community atmosphere of peace and contentment should continue. This peace and contentment is due to the spirit of co-operation which exists. Whatever adjustments therefore may be necessary must be in the nature of improved co-operation within the community rather than elements which introduce a spirit of conflict.

2. The readiness of the average villager to subordinate his interests to those of the larger group or community should be continued as a basis for the development of a more symmetrical relationship.

The abuse of this readiness to subordinate one's interests has led to many of the existing weaknesses of the system. A right use of this spirit should lead to a much richer communal life, resulting in a symmetrical rather than an asymmetrical inter-relationship, as at present.

3. The Panchayat should be given back some of its old powers and have the whole-hearted support of the Central Government.

All students of the Indian village community have recognized the potential strength of a properly constituted Panchayat. And efforts have been made on the part of Provincial Governments to rebuild the old Panchayat system. But like all other resolutions, their success depends on the whole-hearted co-operation of administrative officers, who are responsible for reorganizing the Panchayats. Community autonomy does not always fit in with centralized authority. It often leads to independent community action that may with difficulty be reconciled with central administration plans. And this means awkwardness for the central officers. From the viewpoint of an administrative officer, the easiest way to administer an area is to have it so organized that there will not be any autonomous units which may get out of hand. For this reason more than any other, the *Panchayat* laws have received such half-hearted support from administrative officers.

4. The social and economic advantages made possible through farmers living in a village centre rather than in scattered homes, should be cherished.

The system which has associated with the farmers a group of services such as we find in Karimpur, has enabled the farmers to have satisfactions in intimate social contact, that would not be possible for small groups of farmers or isolated farmers. This relationship has been enriched by common loyalties and has possibilities of even greater variety if loyalty to one's co-workers remains paramount to the accumulation of economic goods.

5. The solidarity of the community establishes units which should be utilized in relation to a central government.

The writer agrees with Radhakamal Mukerjee in his contention that the rural community should be a unit of administration and representatton. And the experience of the West as stated by Sanderson should serve as a warning to the East. Sanderson states, "It is this domination of political life by the modern state which has weakened the local community bond, for the people are citizens of the state and nation, from which come all political sanctions." (Sanderson, Rural Community, page 516.)

6. The two important forces, education and religion, which were instrumental in establishing this system should be utilized to guide and direct its members in future action.

Education and religion were two powerful factors in developing the unified beliefs one finds in Karimpur. If new beliefs are to take the place of the old, they must be brought into the common thinking of the average member of the community in the same way as the old. Education is being strengthened by the Government so that new concepts are rapidly being brought in. Religion must supplement this secular training with its moral sanctions. And the two should be correlated.

The weaknesses of the system should be strengthened and the strength of the system retained. In seeking to do this one must recognize that the Hindu Jajmani System emphasizes solidarity, but does not represent symmetrical inter-relationship for all members. It is communalistic—conservative, built on inequality rather than equality. It is static. It represents a high degree of social and economic organization and control. It is socialistic rather than capitalistic. Its strength is in its solidarity, its altruistic emphasis, its communalistic-conservative nature its concreteness, and its high degree of economic and social organization and control. Its weakness lies in its lack of individual freedom, its limited altruism, its inequality of membership, its static nature and economic inelasticity.

Those who are interested in the problem of rural reconstruction in India need to bear in mind these facts. Indian village communities have the advantage over the West in their existing social solidarity. No false concepts of individualism should be allowed to cause a complete breakdown of these villages. History should serve as a guide, so that rural reconstructionists in India may profit by the mistakes of the West, and build a superior village organization on the existing base of a general recognition of mutual social and economic responsibility.

EVALUATION OF THE HINDU JAJMANI SYSTEM

WHAT IS THERE IN THE SYSTEM THAT IS OF VALUE TO THE WEST?

Some Westerners still feel that "East is East and West is West and ne'er the twain shall meet." Hence the West has nothing to learn from the East. Others think that India is entirely medieval, or that its institutions belong to a primitive agricultural life. As there is an increasing recognition of the values to society of group allegiance, as over against strict individualism, one might learn something in this field from studying the social organization of villagers in India. Here we find group loyalties that have held through centuries. We who have attempted to serve and study Indian village life have found that "if we who come to serve them are prepared to listen as well as to teach we shall find that in exchange for our contribution from the outside world, they have much of value from their own severe schooling to share with us." (Wiser, C. V. and W. H., "Behind Mud Walls," page 112.)

We of the West may therefore learn that peace and contentment in the social and economic relationships of a community are attainable only by integrating one's own aims and purposes with those of the local groups. Absolute individualism cannot lead to social and economic satisfaction and stability. It leads to privileged group license, to unbridled self-interest in business practices, to an insatiate desire for profit and the accumulation of wealth, to emphasis on competition rather than co-operation, and to social and economic disorganization. Just as India is helping us to understand more clearly the Galilean Master's teaching of passive resistance, it can help us to understand His teaching that no man has a right to live entirely unto himself, and that they who are strong are under an ethical obligation to bear the burdens of the weak. Each must work for the common good. Only as we are willing to act on this principle shall we be able to realize most fully a healthy social, economic and political life in our communities of the West.